ENCYCLOPAEDIA OF SPECIAL EDUCATION - VIII

EDUCATION OF CHILDREN WITH SPECIAL NEEDS

By

Dr. G. Lokanadha Reddy
Dean, School of Education and
HRD and Dean Academic Affairs
Dravidian University
Kuppam - 517 426
Chittoor Dist, AP State
(INDIA)

Dr. R. Ramar
Headmaster
S.S.H.N. Hr. Secondary School
Muhavur - 626 111
Tamil Nadu
&

Dr. A. Kusuma
Dept. of Human Development &
Family Studies
Sri Padmavathi Mahila Visvavidyalayam
Tirupati (A.P.)

DISCOVERY PUBLISHING HOUSE PVT. LTD.
NEW DELHI-110 002

Published by:

DISCOVERY PUBLISHING HOUSE PVT. LTD.
4383/4B, Ansari Road, Darya Ganj
New Delhi-110 002 (India)
Phone : +91-11-23279245; 23253475; 43596065
Mobile : +91 9811179893 / +91 9871656464
E-mail : discoverybooksindia@gmail.com
orderdphbooks@gmail.com
web : www.discoverypublishinggroup.com

First Published: **2000**

Reprinted: **2024**

ISBN: 978-81-7141-539-7

Education of Children with Special Needs

Printed at:
Infinity Imaging Systems
Delhi

PREFACE

This book is a general introduction to the characteristics of children with special needs and their education. The book attempts a wide coverage of classroom practices besides covering the psychological, medical and sociological aspects of disabilities. This book is intended to give guidance to the general education classroom teacher as well as to special educators.

The introductory chapter presents an overview of special education and children with special needs. Each of the succeeding seven chapters deals with specific type of impairment Visual impairment, speech and hearing impairment, mental retaidation, slow learning, Learning disabilities, and emotional/behavioural disorders besides giftedness. Each chapter covers the causes of the specific impairment besides enumerating the characteristics of the children with that specific impairment. Also, the chapter provides a detailed description of procedures for identification and outlines the educational programmes for the children with the specific needs. The last chapter introduces the concept of inclusive education to the readers.

Other features of this book are chapter learning objectives that state what the readers should be able to do after reading the chapter and a summary that recaps the main points. Also, references are furnished at the end of each chapter to facilitate readers' supplementary reading. An end of book glossary provides an additional reference tool for students and teachers, as do the book's name index, subject index, and list of references.

This book will be very useful to teachers of both general education and special education. Effective teaching is not a bag of tricks, not a set of abstract principles, but an intelligent application of well understood principles and programmes to solve practical problems in the classroom. We hope this book will help give teachers the intellectual and practical skills needed to do the most important job in the world, that is, teaching the children with special needs.

Authors

CONTENTS

1

SPECIAL EDUCATION AND SPECIAL CHILDREN

OBJECTIVES

This chapter delineates the concept of special children and provides definition and categories of special children. After reading this chapter, the reader should be able to:

1. Understand the concept of special children.
2. Define special children.
3. Know the categories of special children.
4. Develop an insight into visual, hearing and speech impairments.
5. Understand about education for gifted and socially disadvantaged children.

CONCEPT OF SPECIAL EDUCATION

The very term 'Special Education' includes all aspects of education which are applied to special children such as physically handicapped, mentally retarded, disadvantaged and gifted children. These methods are not usually applied for average children and is not a total programme which is entirely different from the education of normal children. It includes those aspects of education which are specific in addition to the regular programmes for all children. In some developed countries like U.S.A and U.K. schools for special children are mostly residential. The different views taken on special education have ignited spark of controversies over segregating some children from the mainstream and providing them with extra opportunities. There are arguments for and against both special education and integrated education.

DEFINITION OF SPECIAL EDUCATION

Special education means specifically designed instruction that meets the unusual needs of special children. It requires special materials, teaching techniques, or equipment and/or facilities. For example, visually impaired children may require reading materials in large print or Braille; hearing impaired children may require hearing aids and/or instruction in sign language; physically disabled students may need special equipments; emotionally disordered children may need smaller and more highly structured classes; and gifted or talented students may require access to working professionals. Special Education, to be effective, warrants related services such as special transportation, psychological assessment, physical and occupational therapy, medical treatment and counselling. The foremost goal of special education is finding and capitalising on special children's abilities.

NEED FOR SPECIAL EDUCATION

It is true that educationally backward children, handicapped children and gifted children are in need of specific facilities for their optimum development. Educators feel the importance of designing special instruction for the benefit of special children.

The proponents of special education put forth the following reasons in support of their argument.

i) Special classes are very essential for educationally backward children because they very much require specific teaching methods to circumvent their deficiency.

ii) A normal classroom generally consists of children who belong to diverse categories such as below average, average, bright, both physically and mentally handicapped, emotionally disturbed, learning disabled and slow learners. A classroom teacher usually finds it very difficult to devise his instruction so as to reach out to all these categories. Hence special education is not only meant to enable the special children to surmount their learning problems but is also conducive for regular classroom teachers.

iii) Education begins where medicine ends. It is of medical concern to provide a hearing aid to hard of hearing children. But teaching the children to use their residual vision or hearing capacities effectively is certainly an educational function. This warrants special education for these children.

iv) It is not possible to ensure optimum human resource development without developing the potentials of special children. Special equipments and additional training are quite, necessary for teaching special children, which are expensive and need adequate budgetary provisions. As a matter of fact, neglect of special children as well as handicapped will be more expensive than providing adequate training. Without special education and/or training these children can not develop independent living skills and social skills and will be more likely to become a liability. So special education for them is indispensable.

v) Special education is very necessary for gifted students also for it provides them with proper stimulation. Generally, a classroom teacher can not provide proper stimulation to both the talented and dull students in the general class. Unlike average children, gifted children are more sensitive and they are quick and alert in thinking. So they need enriched curricular programmes to work to their potentials.

Special education may be imported in the regular classroom, special classroom or in a combination of both. Earlier it was primarily confined to special classes. But now, a special education programme for special children is very much an integral part of general education.

RELATIONSHIP BETWEEN GENERAL EDUCATION AND SPECIAL EDUCATION

During the 1980s the relationship between general and special education became a matter of great concern to policymakers, researchers, and advocates for special children. Educators proposed to change the relationship between general and special education. They made radical calls to restructure or merge the two. This came to be known as regular education initiative (REI). Moderate proponents of REI suggested that general education teachers take more responsibility to teach students with mild or moderate disabilities. Special educators should serve more as consultants or resources person to regular classroom teachers and less special teachers of children. More radical proponents of REI suggested that special education be eliminated as a separate identifiable part of education. They called for a single, unified educational system in which all child must be viewed as unique, special, and entitled to the same quality of education.

Regardless of how one views REI, the controversy about the relationship between special and general education has made the classroom teachers more aware of the problems of decicling just which students should be taught with specific curricula, which students should receive special attention or services, and where and by whom these should be provided. There are no part answers to the questions about how special and general education should work together to ensure that every child receives an appropriate education. However, it is clear that the relationship between general and special education should be one of co-operation and collaboration. They should not become independent or mutually exclusive educational trades. At the same time, it is to be admitted that general and special educators have somewhat different roles to play. With this in mind, the roles to be played by all educators and the special education teacher in particular are summarised below.

ROLE OF ALL EDUCATORS

Hallahan and Kauffman (1991) have clearly outlined the roles of all educators and special educators in educating special children. Whether specifically trained in special education or not, a teacher has to participate in educating special children in any one of the following ways. A high level of professional competence and ethical judgement is required to conform to these expectations.

1. Accommodating Individual Students' Needs

A teacher must take maximum effort to accommodate individual students' needs. There are diverse students in every class. Every teacher must make maximum effort to meet the needs of individuals who may differ in some way from the average or typical student in his or her classroom. Flexibility, adaptation, accommodation, and special education are expected of every teacher. Only when teachers' best possible efforts to meet a student's individual needs become futile, should special education be considered necessary.

2. Assessing Academic Abilities and Disabilities

The psychologists and other special education personnel may administer formal standardised tests to a student. But it is the teacher's assessment of the student's performance in the classroom that stands foremost. Teachers must be able to assess specifically and precisely how far the student is able or unable to perform in all academic areas for which they are responsible.

3. Referring For Evaluation

Teachers must make extensive efforts to screen and identify all handicapped children and youths of school age. They must observe students' behaviour and refer those they suspect of having disabilities or serious problems for evaluation by a multidisciplinary team. A student should not be referred for special education unless all the efforts made by the teacher to accommodate his needs in regular class are unsuccessful.

4. Participating in Eligibility Conferences

Students' eligibility for special education must be determined by an interdisciplinary team before they are provided special education. Teachers must work with other teachers and professionals from other disciplines such as psychology, medicine, or social work to determine a student's eligibility for special education. The class teacher's role in this teamwork should not be underestimated.

5. Writing Individualised Education Programmes

Teachers must have the expertise to write individualised education programmes to eater to the needs of diverse students. Written individualised programmes must be on file in the records of all disabled students. Teachers much participate in conferences in which the programme is formulated. Such conferences can include the student and/or parents, as well as other professionals.

6. Communicating with Parents or Guardians

Teachers must consult with parents or guardians during the evaluation of their children's eligibility for special education, formulation of the individualised education programme, and reassessment of any special programme that may be designed for their children. Teachers must communicate with parents or guardians about their children's /wards' problems, placement, and progress.

7. Collaborating with other Professionals

Teachers must collaborate with other professionals in identifying and making maximum use of exceptional children's abilities. It is not the exclusive responsibility of any one professional group to find and implement solutions to the challenges of educating exceptional children. It is the general and special education teachers who must share the responsibility for educating students with special needs. In addition, teachers must collaborate with other professionals, depending on the students' exceptionality. Professionals like psychologists, physicians, physical therapists and a variety of other specialists rely on the teacher to implement critical aspects of evaluation or treatment.

ROLE OF SPECIAL EDUCATORS

Special educators must be competent enough to perform the aforesaid duties. In addition, they must attain special expertise in the following areas to distinguish them from general educators. Expectations for special education teachers may vary from school system to school system and from state to state. What are listed here are some areas of competence with which every special educator will necessarily be concerned.

1. Expertise to Teach Children with Learning Problems

Most of the students with disabilities or handicaps experience considerable difficulty in learning academic skills. Their sensory impairments, physical disabilities, and mental or emotional disabilities tend to make academic learning more difficult for them. The difficulty may be slight or extreme. Special education teachers must evince patience and hope in dealing with exceptional children. In addition to these requisite qualities, they must have the technical expertise to present academic tasks in such a way that students with disabilities can understand and respond appropriately.

2. Tackling Serious Behaviour Problems

Most of the learning disabled students exhibit behaviours problems in addition to their other exceptionalities. Some of them are in need of special education primarily because of their inappropriate or disruptive behaviour. It therefore requires the special education teachers to have special talent to deal effectively with more than the usual troublesome behaviour of students. In addition to understanding and empathy, they must possess mastery of such techniques that will enable them to draw out particularly withdrawn students, control those who are hyper aggressive and persistently disruptive, and teach critical social skills.

3. Using Technological Advances

Technology plays a predominant role in the education of exceptional children and in improving their daily lives. New devices and techniques are rapidly being developed, particularly for students with sensory and physical disabilities. Special educators must have more than mere awareness of the technology that is available. They must be able to use effectively, evaluate its advantages and disadvantages for teaching the exceptional students with whom they work.

4. Knowledge of Special Education Law

Special education today involves many details of law, particularly in developed countries. In countries like America, disabled students' rights are spelled out in considerable detail in federal and state legislation. The laws, and rules and regulations that accompany them are constantly being interpreted by new court decisions. These court verdicts have widespread implications for the practice of special education. It does not mean that the special education teachers must be expert in law, but they must be aware of the law's requirements and prohibitions. This will enable them to serve as adequate advocates for students with disabilities.

ISSUES AND TRENDS IN SPECIAL EDUCATION

Some issues in special education have remained remarkably constant over the past 100 years despite legislation and litigation. The following are certain issues with which previous generations and our own have struggled.

- How to define specific exceptionalities?
- How to train teachers of children with particular exceptionalities, and
- How to provide public funding for special education programmes.

In fact, every current issue that one are now facing in special education has been a matter of controversy since the beginning. Still, some issues are key concerns of the special educators of

1990s. The following are the most important present day issues and trends in special education.

1. *Normalisation*: - It is very important to ensure that education and everyday living environment of the students with disabilities are as "normal" as possible.
2. *Integration*: - It is very important to educate children with special needs and normal children together so that students will not be separated into ability groups or removed from their normal peer group.
3. *Cultural Diversity*: - It is very imperative for the classroom teacher to recognise and value cultural differences and diversity in the classroom so that "normal" differences associated with a particular culture will not be mistaken for exceptionality.
4. *Early Intervention*: - It is very important to identify exceptionalities or the special needs as early in the children's life as possible so that effective educational programmes can be provided and /or other services can be designed to maximise the child's potential and minimise any disability.
5. *Transition*: - It requires the educators to prepare children with special needs for the world of work and adult living. It includes continued education and career opportunities, so that they can achieve their maximum level of independence and productivity following their high school years.

CONCEPT OF SPECIAL CHILDREN

The study of special children is the study of differences. The special child is different in some way or the other from the average child. In very simple terms, a special child is one who may have problems or special talents in thinking, seeing, hearing, speaking, socialising or moving. A special child has a combination of special abilities or disabilities. These children are either far enough below or far enough above the average range. They need very much specialised attention, which is not provided in regular classrooms.

The study of special children is not markedly different from the average children in every way. Actually, most special children are average in more ways than they are different. Until recently, professionals, and common people simply focused on the differences between special children and average children. They did not focus on the ways in which all children are alike. Now educationists tend to give more attention to what special children and average children have in common i.e., similarities in their characteristics, needs and ways of learning. This has made the study of special children more complex.

In the classroom, children are so distributed that most of them can be classified as average or normal. But there are some students in every classroom who deviate mentally, socially, educationally, physically or culturally from normal children. Such children need special educational care and their learning problems are to be tackled in a special manner. These children are special children and they constitute about a considerable percentage of student population. Educating these children is a challenging task in human resource development.

Special children possess specific disability or special abilities. In the case of gifted children, they have special abilities and they are so far above the average children that they are neglected in the classroom. As these children are much ahead of the average children in the classroom, the teachers do not pay due attention to these students. Also, they do not devise instruction in tune with the capabilities of these students. On the contrary, those students who have specific disability find it very difficult to cope with other children. It warrants employing special methods and means in the instruction of these special children.

DEFINITIONS OF SPECIAL CHILDREN

Special Children are those students who require special education and related services if they are to realise their full human potential. These children are in need of special education because they are markedly different from most children in the classroom in one or more of the following ways. They may have mental retardation, specific learning difficulties, emotional problems, physical disabilities hampering their learning, disordered speech or language, or special gifts or talents. So special children are those children who differ from the average to such an extent that their differences warrant some type of special instruction, either within the regular classroom or in special classes.

Some special children learn to live with their disabilities or special abilities in such ways that surprise most of us. Their differences from most people do not keep them from leading full and normal lives as children or as adults. Sometimes special education plays no role in their lives because their abilities, motivation, and support from their families and communities are sufficient to allow them to circumvent their deficiencies without special assistance. But this is not the case with most of the special children and they need special assistance to realise their full human potential.

The term "special" is applied to a trait or to a person possessing the trait if there is a considerable extent of deviation from the normal possession of that trait. These special children differ from the average to such an extent that their differences warrant some type of special instruction either in the mainstream or in special schools. The difference in the case of special children is only one of degree. The difference lies in learning or behaviour of the child. For example, many students may have vision or hearing impairment, but most of these cases can be corrected with glasses and hearing aids. Only a few may require special helps like large print, magnifiers or Braille materials. Such students who need special instruction can be categorised under special children.

DIFFERENCE BETWEEN DISABILITY AND HANDICAP

Though we use the term 'handicapped' to refer to individuals with disabilities, there is an important distinction between disability and handicap. A disability is an inability to do something. It is a diminished capacity to perform in a specific way. A handicap, on the other hand, is a disadvantage imposed on an individual. A disability may or may not be a handicap, depending on the circumstances. Similarly, a handicap may or may not be caused by a disability. For example, blindness is a disability that can be anything but a handicap in the dark. In fact, in the dark the person who is not blind is handicapped while the actual blind can move about as usual. Usually, people handicap persons who are different from themselves by stereotyping them or not giving them an opportunity to do the things they are able to do. So we must constantly strive to separate the disability from the handicap. That is, our goal should be to confine their handicap to those characteristics that can not be changed. We should not impose any further handicap by our attitudes or our unwillingness to accommodate their disability.

CATEGORIES OF SPECIAL CHILDREN

All the special children can be classified into two broad categories as the handicapped and gifted. Again the handicapped special children can further be classified on the basis of their specific handicaps. Their specific handicaps may be due to physical attributes, mental attributes, or socio-cultural attributes. Under each subgroup, there are two more specific handicaps. The following classification can be made taking the above discussion of special children into consideration.

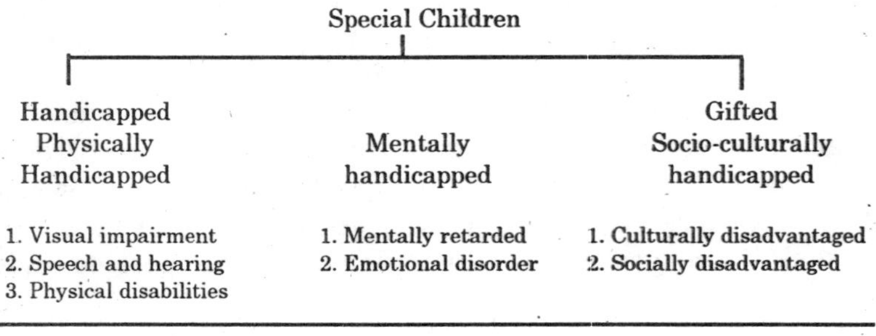

Educationists have classified special children into many broad categories each of them having one or more types. But in our discussion we follow the above flow chart. The two broad categories and some of the major types are discussed below.

HANDICAPPED CHILDREN

All the handicapped children are special children. This category is generally known as physically handicapped children. A physically handicapped person is an individual who is afflicted with a physical impairment which, in some way or the other, limits or inhibits his participation in normal educational activities. In simple words, any person having a disability is called handicapped person. Sometimes the handicap may be caused by mental and socio-cultural attributes. A disability is an outcome of an objectively defined impairment of structure or function. For example, the loss of vision in one eye or the loss of hearing in one ear is a disability.

How far the disability handicaps its possessor largely depends upon the circumstances. There are certain disabilities that do not really operate as a handicap. For example, colour blindness is a handicap for those who are in the profession of navigation or driving. But if they are placed in a job, which does not require colour vision, colour blindness may not be a handicap at all. Stammering is a handicap. For an orator or lawyer stammering is a handicap. But a stammerer can be a good writer or scientist. Also, some of the disabilities can be mitigated with the aid of sophisticated instruments like hearing aids and self-propelled chairs of paraplegics.

Generally a handicap is a partial disability. In special children the disability usually affects one organ, sense or system, the rest remaining impaired, or being even better than the average. The handicap does not necessarily reduce the entire power. For example, a blind with visual impairment may have strong legs, but he will have considerable difficulty in walking in unfamiliar places. It is important to note that some disabilities can produce secondary handicaps. For example, a child who has normal speech but other severe defects is likely to have speech defects.

Now we will discuss some specific physical handicaps found in children.

(i) Visually Impaired Children

There are two most common ways of describing visual impairment. They are the legal and educational definitions. The former one is used by the lay people and the practitioners in the medical profession; the latter is favoured by the educators.

A legally blind person is one who has visual acuity of 20/200 or less in the better eye even with correction (e.g., eyeglasses) or has a field of vision so narrow that its widest diameter subtends an angular distance no greater than 20 degrees. The fraction 20/200 means that the person can see at 20 feet what a person with normal vision can see at 200 feet. In addition to this medical classification of blindness, there is also a category referred to as partially sighted. According to the legal classification system, partially sighted individuals have visual acuity falling between 20/70 and 20/200 in the better eye with correction.

Many professionals, particularly educators, have found the legal classification scheme inadequate. They are of the opinion that visual acuity is not a very accurate predictor of how people will function or use whatever remaining sight they possess. According to educational definition blind individuals are those who are so visually impaired that they must learn to read Braille or use aural methods. Educators often refer to those visually impaired individuals who can be read print, even if they need magnifying devices or large-print books, as having low vision.

Most of the visual problem is the result of errors of refraction. Because of faulty structure and/or malfunction of the eye, the light rays do not focus on the retina. The most common visual impairments are myopia (nearsightedness) heperopia (farsightedness), and astigation (blurred vision). Eyeglasses or contact lenses can usually correct these problems. Most serious visual impairments in school age students are due to hereditary factors. Blindness is also caused by certain environmental as well as genetic agents. These etiological agents include infections, diseases, accidents, poisoning, tumours and cancer.

Visual impairment may result in a few subtle language differences but not in deficient language skills. Blindness does not result in intellectual retardation. Visually impaired children rely more on touch than on vision to learn about their world. So there are some differences in conceptual development. Sight facilitates better perception of objects or parts of an object simultaneously whereas touch results in successive perceptions of most objects and requires more conscious effort. Early training in use of strategies helps children use their touch more efficiently.

Personality problems are not an inherent condition of visual impairment. Any social adjustment problems of blind individuals are primarily the result of society's reaction to the blind. The stereotypies (e.g. repetitive rocking) exhibited by a few blind individuals can be an impediment to social acceptance; but behavioural techniques can diminish their occurrence.

Educational experiences in regular classrooms are frequently visual. But with some modifications in methods, teachers can apply the same general principles of instruction to both sighted and visually impaired students. Braille may be useful for those whose vision is so impaired that they can not read even large type. More and more blind individuals are turning to audiotapes for their reading medium. The compressed speech method, in particular, permits fast and efficient presentation of material. Also, there are a number of technological devices being developed for the visually impaired population. Some of them are optician, the Kurzwell Reading Machine, and talking calculators.

Most scientists believe that the most important ability for successful adjustment of visually impaired people is mobility. Mobility training can involve the use of human guides, guide dogs, the long cane, and electronic devices such as the sonicguide. Most mobility instructors recommend the long cane for the majority of blind people.

The four basic educational placements for visually impaired children are the residential school, special class, resource room, and itinerant teacher. More and more visually impaired students are in general education classrooms. Residential placement, at one time the most popular alternative, is now recommended infrequently. Current trend is for integrating programming between residential and community based facilities. Education for the adolescent and adult stresses independent living and employment skills. Independence is extremely difficult to achieve for some visually impaired people, but it is extremely important, especially for work adjustment, for them to be able to function independently. A contributing factor to dependency is society, which often mistakenly views visually impaired people as helpless.

Only about one third of working-age blind adults are employed, and they are frequently overqualified for their jobs. Professionals are now attempting to change this bleak employment picture with innovative approaches such as job training in regular work settings rather than simulated setting in classrooms.

2. Hearing Impaired Children

Hearing influences learning and other aspects of maturation. If a child hears imperfectly, there is every possibility that he will speak incorrectly. Auditory defects can be found in one or both ears. Sometimes children have no power of hearing at all. Some terms are used to denote auditory impairments. These are 'deaf' 'hard of hearing', 'partially deaf', and 'deaf mute'.

In defining hearing impairments, professionals with an educational orientation are concerned primarily with the extent to which the hearing loss affects the ability to speak and understand spoken language. The time of onset is therefore important.

Prelingual deafness: Those who are deaf at birth or before spoken language develops are referred to as having Prelingual deafness.

Postlingual deafness: Those who acquire their deafness after spoken language starts to develop are referred to as having postlingual deafness.

Hard of hearing: Those who lose their hearing after they acquire speech are known as hard of hearing.

Congenitally deaf: Those who are born deaf are known as congenitally deaf.

Adventitiously deaf: Those who are born with normal hearing but later lose it are called adventitious deaf 'Hard of hearing' children have slight, marginal and moderate losses. They can be educated through the auditory channel.

TYPES OF HEARING DEFECTS

The hearing impaired children can be subdivided according to the organic hearing loss. These are as follows:

(i) Conductive Hearing Loss

Conductive losses are impairments that interfere with transferral of sound along the conductive pathway. This is the most common hearing impairment among children. In this case there is reduction in the loudness of sound so that its clarity is distorted. This often results from pathological changes in the middle ear due to congenital or acquired defects of the ear. If it is mild, then a surgical or medical remedy is possible. Proper and timely treatment of acute infections in the middle ear and the prevention of chronic infections of the ear will often greatly reduce incidence of hearing defects. Hearing aids and sound amplification systems are also conducive to mitigate conductive defects.

(ii) Sensorineural Hearing Loss

Sensorineural problems are confined to the complex inner ear and are apt to be much harder to treat. The most common causes of inner ear troubles are linked to hereditary factors. Acquired hearing losses of the inner ear include those due to bacterial infections such as meningitis, viral infections, such as mumps and measles, prenatal infections of the mother such as cytomegalovirus maternal rubella, and syphilis, and deprivation of oxygen at birth. Here, the sound is conducted without any difficulty, properly. Hearing aids, auditory training, lip-reading and language training can help children having moderate defects. However, special schooling is needed for children with profound hearing impairments.

(iii) Psychogenic Hearing Loss

Here, the cause of the difficulty is purely psychological. Very often, there is a history of ear infection, which appears to act as a shock organ for localisation of the psychic symptom. Sometimes, under a stressful situation, the child may unconsciously develop hearing loss as an escape from what according to him is an intolerable situation. It is very difficult to distinguish between organic defects and psychogenic losses. Appropriate audiological techniques and meticulous observation can often help to bring out a correct diagnosis.

(iv) Central Auditory Defects

These defects are extremely complex. Their causes and pathogenesis are not known. Children having this defect are aware of sound but they are unable to get its meaning. These defects cause severe communication problems. During early infancy, use of certain life saving drugs can also affect auditory system. Such children require an extensive and prolonged therapy because they are difficult to manage.

Hearing impaired pupils can be found in a variety of settings, ranging from general education classrooms to residential settings. Mainstreaming of hearing impaired students is growing in popularity; but only about 20 percent of hearing impaired students are placed primarily in regular classrooms. A growing minority believes that mainstreaming is not appropriate for deaf students. The language problems exhibited by many learning disabled students is major deterrent to widespread integration into general education classrooms.

(iii) Speech Impaired Children

Communication is an essential feature of interaction. Language is a must for human interaction. Many people confuse 'speech' with 'language'. When the speech of an individual differs significantly from that of others and it affects communication, it is diagnosed as speech defects. The number of children suffering from speech defects is much more than the number of those having any other impairment.

Development of speech and language depends on speech mechanism and the psychological environment the child lives in. Physical, social and psychological conditions very much affect the normal development of a child. These developments can affect the development of the speech and language skills of the child ultimately.

TYPES OF SPEECH DEFECTS

The classification of speech defects is based on purpose of classification. Speech defects may be classified according to such major symptoms as articulation disorders, voice disorders, delayed speech, stammering and disturbances of rhythm. These can also be classified on the basis of cause according to which it may be organic or functional. But this dichotomy does not hold good for various reasons. Now we shall discuss some of the major speech defects in detail.

(i) Disorders of Articulation

This type of disorder includes various symptoms such as distortion, omission, addition or substitution of speech sounds. Very often it includes mispronunciation of an entire word or words. These defects are commonly found among children. According to statistics, 70 to 80 percent of speech defects are of this kind. In young children, this defect manifests as immature speech. However, it is possible to circumvent this deficiency.

(ii) Disorders of Voice (Phonation)

This type of disorder is found more often in adults than in children. It includes marked deviations in terms of loudness, quality, pitch or intensity of sounds. In addition, some other anomalies like breathings, huskiness, nasality and hoarseness are also found. The causes may be emotional, vocal abuse, overuse or infections. Tension and shocks in life are also contributory factors.

iii) Delayed Speech

Among children, the frequency of delayed speech is much higher than any other defects in communication. The chief causes of delayed speech are hearing loss, mental retardation, cerebral dysfunction, emotional disturbances and environmental deprivation. Very often, children are not able to speak at the usual age due to lack of motivation. Professional help should be sought for the treatment and diagnosis of delayed speech.

iv) Stuttering and Stammering

Stuttering is a type of repetitive speech. Very often stuttering is confused with stammering. These are most serious forms of speech disorders. They are chiefly caused by emotional difficulties, fear of failure, fear of authority, anxiety, frustration, insecurity, hostility, overprotection by adults, etc. Ridiculing the children will aggravate the situation.

While stuttering is often considered a disorder of rhythm, stammering is marked by a difficulty in producing any speech sound. In both the cases the affected children need to be treated by a specialist. There are two approaches for the treatment of stammering i.e. symptomatic treatment and psychotherapy.

MENTALLY RETARDED CHILDREN

Generally, mental retardation is regarded as a disease. Earlier some people described it as a condition. In the past, the mentally retarded children were neglected by the society as they were thought to be possessed by spirits. Now a day, there is greater acceptance of and awareness about mentally retarded children among the general public.

The first standard definition of mental retardation was proposed by Hebber (1962) taking intelligence, adaptive behaviour and developmental level into consideration. Then a more adequate definition was developed by the American Association of Mental Deficiency (AAMD) in 1973. It states; "Mental retardation refers to significantly sub-average general intellectual functioning existing concurrently with deficits in adaptive behaviour and manifested during developmental period". This developmental period includes the life span from birth to 18 years of age.

AAMD CLASSIFICATION OF MENTAL RETARDATION

The most commonly accepted approach to classification is to consider retarded children according to degree of severity. AAMD classifies mental retardation as mild, moderate, severe, and profound. These terms help minimise negative stereotyping. Some educators also use the classifications educable, trainable, and severely and profoundly retarded.

CLINICAL CLASSIFICATION OF MENTAL RETARDATION

Taking I.Q. into consideration, the following classification has been made by psychologists.

Level of mental Retardation	Wechsler IQ	Stanford Binet I.
i. Mild	(55 - 69)	(52 - 67)
ii. Moderate	(40 - 54)	(36 - 51)
iii. Severe	(25 - 30)	(20 - 35)
iv. Profound	Under 25	Under 20

Clinical evidences indicate that on an average 2.5 per cent of children in India are mild to moderately mentally retarded and 0.5 per cent severely retarded.

CAUSES OF MENTAL RETARDATION

A variety of factors can cause mental retardation. Most people with mild retardation are considered culturally - familially retarded. Environment and /or heredity factors are the main causes of mild retardation. We can categorise causes of moderately to severely retarded individuals as due to genetic factor or brain damage. Down syndrome, PKU, and Tay-Sachs disease are all examples of genetic causes. Brain damage can be the result of infectious diseases such as meningitis, encephalitis, rubella, and pediatric AIDS. Premature birth can also result in mental retardation.

EDUCATIONAL PROBLEMS OF MENTALLY RETARDED

Individuals with mental retardation have learning problems related to attention memory language and academics. In metracognition they lack depth of processing and executive control. Depth of processing refers to how much cognitive activity a person has to undergo to perform a task. Mentally retarded individuals process information at a shallower level than non-retarded people do. Executive control refers to the ability in planning, monitoring, and evaluating one's own performance. Individuals with retardation have problems with executive control processes. In addition to cognitive problems, mentally retarded children often have behavioural and personality problems, which also aggravate learning problems.

EDUCATION FOR MENTALLY RETARDED

Educational goals for mildly and moderately retarded students are quite similar. At younger ages there is an emphasis on readiness skills, and at older ages, there is more emphasis on functional academics and vocational training. Functional academics are academics for the purpose of enabling the person to function independently. Educational programmes for severely and profoundly retarded students are characterised by (1) age appropriate curriculum and materials, (2) functional activities, (3) community - based instruction, (4) therapy, (5) interaction with nondisabled students, and (6) integrating the family environment. Applied behavioural analysis is often the method of choice for teachers working with retarded students.

GIFTED CHILDREN

Disagreements about definitions of giftedness centre around the questions of exactly how gifted children are superior; how this superiority is measured, the degree to which the individual must be superior to be considered gifted; and who should make up the comparison group. Even the terms used can be confusing. Gifted children are those whose cognitive abilities place them in the upper 3 to 5 per cent of the population. The gifted children have an I.Q of 130 or above. These children have superior ability, creativeness in thinking and superior talent in specific domains.

Giftedness may be defined as demonstration of high ability, high creativity, and high task commitment. Therefore, a given child may be gifted at one time, in one area of performance, or in one situation and not in another. Giftedness is not an absolute, fixed human characteristic. Furthermore, it can be defined to include many or only very few people. Consequently the prevalence of giftedness cannot be precisely established. Perhaps 15 to 25 percent of the population has the potential for exhibiting gifted behaviour at some time during their schooling in at least one area of performance.

FACTORS PROMOTING GIFTEDNESS

Genetic factors are known to contribute significantly to behavioural development, including intelligence and gifted performance. Environmental factors-families; schools and communities-are also known to influence the development of giftedness. Giftedness, then, is a result of combined biological and environmental influences - nature and nurture. Current research suggests that one's collection of genes sets limits of performance; the actual performance within those limits is determined by environmental factors.

ATTITUDE TOWARDS GIFTED CHILDREN AND THEIR EDUCATION

In recent years interest in education of gifted children has increased, but most gifted students do not receive any special services appropriate to their abilities. As a result, some of the gifted students become under achievers those who fail to achieve at a level consistent with their abilities, whatever the reason. Underachievement is often a problem of minority students, whose special abilities tend to be overlooked because of biased expectations and/or the values of majority.

Generally gifted children, when allowed to attend regular classes, face a lot of problems of their own. An average class and its programmes are planned for children of average ability. By admitting gifted children into this class, they are denied the opportunity they need for full development of their talents. Their education is restricted. The teacher finds himself placed in a very awkward position as to how to satisfy both the talented and the average children.

Giving double promotion is no solution. When the gifted child is given an accelerated promotion, he is placed out of his own group with respect to physical, social, and emotional development. In such situation, the gifted child may find himself out of step in other activities and interests. Therefore, the gifted children should be provided with an enriched programme while they are allowed to share the experiences of children of their own level of development. A gifted child always wants to accomplish difficult tasks, which poses a challenge to him and which he can complete independently.

EDUCATION OF GIFTED CHILDREN

Education of gifted and talented students should have three characteristics. First, the curriculum should be designed to accommodate advanced cognitive skills. Secondly instructional strategies should be designed so as to be consistent with learning styles in particular curriculum area. Lastly, there must be administrative facilitation of grouping for instruction neglected.

Programmes and practices in the education of gifted students are extremely varied and include special schools, acceleration, special classes, tutoring, and enrichment during the school year or summer. Administrative plans for modifying the curriculum include enrichment in the classroom, use of consultant teachers, resource rooms, community mentors, independent study, special classes and special schools. Acceleration has not been popular plan for educating gifted students, although considerable research supports it. A major issue is acceleration versus enrichment. Programmes of acceleration especially in mathematics, in which student's skip grades or complete college level work easily, have been evaluated positively.

Models of enrichment include a "revolving door" plan in which students continue to engage in enrichment activities for as long as they are able to go beyond the usual curriculum of their age mates and a school wide enrichment model that is designed to improve the learning environment for all students. Although the gifted students do not face any problem in their transitions to adolescence, adulthood, and higher education and employment, many of them do need personal and career counselling and guidance in making contacts with school and community resources.

SOCIALLY DISADVANTAGED CHILDREN

Deprivation, in ecological terms, consists of two-tier concentric layer (1) The upper and more visible layer contains home, school, peer group etc., each providing three dimensions: Physical space and materials, social roles and relationships and activities, and (ii) The supporting or the surrounding layer is provided by geographic and physical environment and the institutional setting of the general services and amenities. Of course, this scheme provides a better conceptualisation of various kinds of deprivation.

Again, cultural deprivation refers to a complex set of condition, which create intellectual deficiency in a child. These conditions include unstimulated environment, lack of verbal interaction with adults, poor sensory experience and other deleterious environmental factors associated with poverty.

SCHEDULED CASTES AND SCHEDULED TRIBES AS SOCIALLY DISADVANTAGED

In India, Scheduled Castes and Scheduled Tribes constitute a special group of disadvantaged community. Articles 341 and 342 of the Indian Constitution deal with protection and safeguards of SCs and STs. These SCs-STs constitute about 25 per cent of the total population of India. The all-India rates of SCs and STs were 21.38 per cent and 16.85 per cent respectively according to 1981 census. The progress of the education of women of these communities is significantly poor. The literacy rates of women of SC and ST were 10.93 per cent and 8.04 per cent as against

29.43 per cent of other population sectors. However, the progress of higher education in these communities is significantly low.

CHARACTERISTICS OF SOCIALLY DISADVANTAGED CHILDREN

The socially disadvantaged children are marked by the following three general characteristics during their school years. They are:

1) Progressive decline in intellectual functioning
2) Cumulative academic achievement deficits
3) Premature school termination or higher dropout rate

These characteristics are discussed in detail in a later chapter.

CAUSES OF LOW ACHIEVEMENT

Research evidences reveal that high caste and scheduled caste students differ significantly in academic achievement. The lower achievement of the socially disadvantaged children can be ascribed to at least five causes such as:

i) Malnutrition
ii) Genetic factors
iii) Lack of stimulating early experience
iv) Social motivations, and
v) Cultural values

However, the cognitive style or strategy adopted by a group also can account for the lower performance of the disadvantaged children.

EDUCATION FOR SOCIALLY DISADVANTAGED CHILDREN

Educational provisions have been made for the socially disadvantaged children by the government. In the area of intellectual and social competence, enrichment programmes are designed to develop and enlarge children's conceptual repertoire and communicative skills. Some important measures are discussed below.

i) Establishment of Residential Schools

Appropriate steps should be taken to establish residential schools and Ashram schools for disadvantaged students like SC and ST students. Of course, residential schools should be made to suit the needs of Adivasis. Measures should be taken to make these institutions more homely.

ii) Financial Help

Poverty is a pertinent factor, which serves as a barrier in the path of progress of socially disadvantaged children. Both central and state governments have been giving financial aid to these students since long in the form of pre-matric and post-matric scholarships. They are exempted from paying admission and tuition fees also.

iii) Appointment of Expert Teachers

Teachers who specialise in tribal dialect should be appointed. Residential accommodation must be provided to teaching experts and administrators who work in hilly and tribal areas. Inservice training programmes and refresher courses should be conducted periodically.

iv) Craft Education

Useful crafts like carpentry, weaving and tailoring must be introduced to suit the needs of SC and ST students, which are indispensable for their economic development. According to educational statistics, craft education is compulsory in some states and union territories.

v) Adjustment of School Hours and Vocations

There must be an adjustment of school vocations and school hours for these students so that they can meet the socio-economic needs of the community. The percentage of dropouts and stagnation can be diminished to a considerable extent if school hours and vocations can be properly adjusted. Also, these students will get ample opportunity to assist their parents.

The above discussed points must be carefully considered and absorbed into the educational strategy for the education of the socially disadvantaged children, so that they will not become victims of cumulative deprivation.

EDUCATION AND CULTURAL DIVERSITY

India is a land known for diverse people and diverse culture. Paradoxically, another strength has been the melding of this diversity into a single, uniquely Indian identity. To understand the implications of cultural diversity for special education, we must first consider the definition of culture and how it is related to the educational needs of children.

Culture is consisting primarily of the symbolic, ideational, and intangible aspects of human societies. Culture includes values and behavioural styles, languages and dialects, non-verbal communication, awareness of one's own cultural distinctiveness, frames of reference, and identification. These elements together make up a national or shared culture, which is referred to as macro culture. Within a national macro culture are found many micro cultures such as ethnic, social, gender, religions, exceptionality and other groups. A person may belong to a variety of micro cultures that affect his or her behaviour.

The general purposes of multicultural education are to promote understanding of micro cultures and foster positive attitudes towards cultural diversity. Ethnic and exceptionality groups are particularly important micro cultures in special education. Multicultural education should ensure that ethnicity and exceptionality are not confused. It should also promote understanding of the micro culture of exceptionality and its relationship to other micro cultures. Educators should design activities to reduce prejudice and stereotyping of multicultural groups other than one's own.

Authorities now recognise the importance of acknowledging students' cultural styles while providing effective instruction in the skills that will enable them to be successful in the dominant culture. Socialisation involves helping students become comfortable with their identification with micro cultural groups, avoid destructive and stereotypic social perceptions and interactions, and become advocates for themselves and other members of their micro cultures. Teachers must become comfortable with their own micro cultural identification and provide classroom activities that encourage understanding.

SUMMARY

The very term special education includes all aspects of education applied to special children such as physically handicapped, mentally retarded disadvantaged and gifted children. These methods are not usually applied for average and normal children. At the same time, special education is not a total programme which is entirely different from the education of normal children. It includes some specific aspects of education in addition to the regular programmes for all children.

Special education is very important to ensure optimum human resource development. Special children very much require specific teaching methods to circumvent their deficiency. A classroom teacher finds it very difficult to devise his instruction so as to reach out to all categories of students. Hence the need for special education.

The controversy about the relationship between special and general education has made the classroom teachers more aware of the problems of deciding just which students should be taught with specific curricula, which students should receive special attention or services, and where and by whom these should be provided. General education and special education should not become independent or mutually exclusive educational tracks. They have somewhat different roles to play.

There are some students in every classroom who deviate mentally, socially, educationally, physically or culturally from normal children. Such children need special educational care and their learning problems are to be tackled in special manner. These children are special children and they constitute about a considerable percentage of student population. Educating these children is a challenging task in human resource development.

Visually impaired children, speech and hearing impaired children, mentally retarded children, slow learners, learning disabled children, emotionally disturbed children and gifted children are some categories of special children. It is very essential to reach out to all these categories of students in order to bring about optimum human resource development.

REFERENCES

Blake K.A. (1976) "*The Mentally Retarded: An Educational Psychology*", Prentice Hall, New Delhi.

Chintamani Kar (1992) "*Exceptional Children: Their Psychology and Instruction*". Sterling Publishers Private Ltd, New Delhi.

Daniel P. Hallahan and James M.Kauffman (1991) "*Exceptional Children - Introduction to Special Education*", Prentice Hall International (U.K) Limited, London.

Jangira, N. K. and others (1988) "*Source book for Teaching Visually Disabled Children*", NCERT, New Delhi.

Uday Shankar (1984) "*Exceptional Children*", Sterling Publishers, New Delhi.

Usha S.Rao (1984) "*Exceptional Children*", Sterling Publishers, New Delhi.

2

VISUALLY IMPAIRED CHILDREN

OBJECTIVES

This chapter deals with visually impaired children. It also provides practical guidelines to practitioners to teach visually impaired children. After reading this chapter, the readers should be able to:

1. Define visual impairment according to legal or medical consideration and educational consideration.
2. Understand the causes and categories of visual impairment.
3. Identify visually impaired children in order to make appropriate assessment and placement.
4. Develop an insight into how to instruct visually impaired children
5. Know the utility and availability of special instructional materials devised for visual impaired children.

Like anyone with a disability, the blind person wants to be treated like everyone else. Most blind people do not seek pity or even unnecessary help. Although they may need assistance in some situations, mostly they prefer to be reminded of their similarities rather than differences.

DEFINITION OF VISUAL IMPAIRMENT

There are two ways of describing visual impairment. One is legal definition and the other is educational definition. The former one is used by lay people and those in the medical profession; the latter is used by the educators.

LEGAL DEFINITION

The legal definition is based on assessment of visual acuity and field of vision. A person is said to be legally blind if he has visual acuity of 20/200 or less in the better eye even with correction or has a field of vision so narrow that its widest diameter subtends an angular distance no greater than 20 degrees. The fraction of 20/200 means that the person sees at 20 feet what a person with normal vision sees at 200 feet. Normal vision acuity is thus 20/20.

There is also another category referred to as partially sighted. According to the legal classification system, partially sighted individuals are those who have visual acuity falling between 20/70 and 20/200 in the better eye with correction (e.g., eyeglasses)

EDUCATIONAL DEFINITION

Most professionals especially educators have found the legal classification system inadequate. According to them visual acuity is not a very accurate predictor of how people will function or use whatever remaining sight they have. It is to be noted that only a small percentage of legally blind people have absolutely no vision, but the vast majority are able to see. According to research evidences only 18 percent of legally blind students are totally blind whereas most individuals classified as legally blind can see well enough to read large or regular print books.

The limitations of legal definition of blindness and partial sightedness led the educators to evolve their own definition. Educational definition is based on the method of reading instruction. For educational purpose, blind people are those individuals whose vision is so severely impaired that they must learn to read Braille or use aural methods such as audiotapes and records. (Braille is a system of raised dots by which blind people "read" with their fingertips and it consists of quadrangular cells containing from one to six dots whose arrangement denotes different letters and symbols.) Those visually impaired individuals who can read print, even if they need magnifying devices or large print books, are referred to as having low vision.

CAUSES OF VISUAL IMPAIRMENT

There are various causes of visual impairment. They are:

i) Errors of refraction
ii) Glaucoma, Cataracts, and diabetes
iii) Prenatal causes
iv) improper muscle functioning

i) Errors of Refraction

The most common visual problems are the result of errors of refraction. Myopia (near sightedness), hyperopia (far sightedness), and astigmatism (Blurred vision) are all examples of refraction errors that affect central visual acuity. Each of these can be serious enough to cause significant impairment. Myopia and hyperopia are the most common impairments of low vision. In these cases, glasses or contact lenses can bring vision within normal limits.

When the eyeball is too long, the light rays from the object would be in focus in front of rather than on the retina. This results in myopia, which affects vision for distant objects, but close vision may be unaffected. When the eyeball is too short, the light rays from the object would be in focus behind rather than on the retina. This results in hyperopia, which affects vision for close objects, but far vision may be unaffected. When the cornea or lens of the eye is irregular, the light rays from the object would be blurred or distorted. This results in astigmatism (blurred vision).

ii) Glaucoma, Cataract, and Diabetic Retinopathy

Glaucoma, cataract and diabetes cause more serious impairments. These occur primarily in adults, but each of them, particularly the latter two can occur in children also.

Glaucoma is a condition in which there is excessive pressure in the eyeball. Left untreated, the condition progresses to the point at which the blood supply to the optic nerve is cut off and blindness results. The cause of glaucoma is presently unknown and its onset can be sudden or very gradual. A common complaint during early stages of glaucoma is that lights appear to have halos around them.

Cataracts are caused by a clouding of lens of the eye, which results in blurred vision. In children the condition is called congenital cataracts. It affects distance and colour vision seriously. Surgery can usually correct the problems caused by cataracts.

Diabetic retinopathy is caused by diabetes. When there is interference with the blood supply to the retina, this condition occurs.

iii) Prenatal causes

There are several other visual impairments that primarily affect children. Visual impairments of school-age children are often due to prenatal causes, many of which are hereditary. Like congenital cataracts and glaucoma, there are other congenital conditions.

Coloboma, another congenital condition, is a degenerative disease in which the central and/or peripheral areas of the retina are not completely formed. This results in impairment of the visual field and/or central visual acuity.

Retinitis Pigmentosa is yet another prenatal condition. It is a hereditary disease resulting in degeneration of retina. Retinitis pigmentosa causes the person's field of vision to narrow.

Also included in the prenatal category are infectious diseases that affect the unborn child, such as syphilis and rubella.

iv) Improper Muscle Functioning

Improper muscle functioning causes two other conditions, which result in visual problems.

Strabismus is a condition in which the eye(s) is (are) directed inward (crossed eyes) or outward. If it is left untreated, strabismus will result in permanent blindness because the brain will eventually reject signals from a deviating eye. Fortunately, most cases of strabismus can be corrected with eye exercises or surgery.

Nystagmus is a condition in which there are rapid involuntary movements of the eyes. This results in dizziness and nausea. Nystagmus is sometimes a sign of brain malfunctioning and /or inner ear problems.

CHARACTERISTICS OF VISUALLY IMPAIRED CHILDREN

There are some psychological and behavioural characteristics pertaining to visually impaired children. These characteristics are discussed below.

i) Restricted language Development

Many authorities believe that lack of vision does not alter very significantly the ability to understand and use language. However, there are a few subtle differences in the way in which language usually develops in visually impaired children compared to sighted children. Blind children's early language tends to be somewhat restricted by their lack of visual experiences. Sighted children use language more readily to refer to activities involving other people and objects whereas visually impaired children's language tends to be most self-centred. It warrants as rich an exposure as possible at as young an age as possible for visually impaired children.

ii) Lag in conceptual Development

Visually impaired children lag behind their sighted peers in conceptual development. There are some important differences between blind and sighted individuals' conceptual development most of which are due to the difference between tactual and visual experiences.

iii) Tactual Perception

The tactual sense is primarily how the blind child acquires a variety of concepts that the sighted child usually acquires through the visual sense. There are two kinds of tactual perceptions. They are synthetic touch and analytic touch.

Synthetic touch refers to a person's tactual exploration of objects small enough to be enclosed by one or both hands. Most physical objects are too large for synthetic touch to be useful.

Analytic touch involves touching of various parts of an object and then mentally constructing these separate parts. The sighted person is able to perceive different objects or the parts of one object simultaneously whereas the blind person must perceive things successively. Blind people are at a distinct disadvantage because they are unable to use sight to help them develop integrated concepts.

iv) Obstacle Sense

A large part of blind person's skill in mobility is the ability to detect physical obstructions in the environment. A blind person walking along the street often seems to be able to "sense" an object in his or her path. This ability has come to be known as obstacle sense. Many lay people and some professionals have taken it to mean that blind people somehow develop an extra sense, but this is not true. Although the obstacle sense is important for mobility of a blind person, it can not by itself make its user a highly proficient traveller. It is just an aid. Also, it requires walking at a fairly slow speed to be able to react in time.

v) Difficulty in Social Skills

It is society's reaction to the blind persons that determines their social adjustment or lack of it. Visually impaired children are not accepted by nondisabled persons because some of them experience difficulty in attaining certain social skills, such as exhibiting appropriate facial expressions. Teaching social skills to visually impaired children will be a very challenging task because such skills are traditionally acquired through modelling and feed back using sight.

vi) Stereotypic Behaviours

An impediment to good social adjustment for a few visually impaired individuals is stereotypic behaviours or stereotypic. These are repetitive, stereotyped movements such as rocking or rubbing the eyes. Stereotypic behaviours are caused by sensory deprivation, social deprivation and retreat to familiar patterns of behaviour under stress.

CATEGORIES OF VISUALLY IMPAIRED CHILDREN

From the definitions given in the beginning section of this chapter one can understand that there are two categories of visually impaired children. They are

i) Totally blind children
ii) Children having low vision

i) Totally Blind Children

Totally blind children are those who are born without ability to see or they must have gone blind by accident, operations etc. According to legal/medical consideration, children who have visual acuity of 20/200 or less in the better eye even with correction (e.g., eyeglasses) are known as totally blind children.

According to educators, those children whose visions are so severely impaired that they must learn to read Braille or use aural methods are known as totally blind children. Total blindness can be recognised easily and identified early, but a detailed examination is needed to identify children having low vision.

ii) Children Having Low Vision

According to medical consideration, this category children are referred to as partially sighted children. They have visual acuity falling between 20/70 and 20/200 in the better eye with correction. According to educators, those visually impaired children who can read print, even if they need magnifying devices or large-print books, are referred to as children having low vision. The detection of low vision is a much more difficult, proposition. Such children have little concept of "vision". As such it is difficult for them to report about their visual problems.

PROBLEMS OF VISUALLY IMPAIRED CHILDREN

The visually impaired children experience many problems like behaviour problems, problems of learning, problems of their placement in society or problems of social adjustment. Some of these problems are discussed below.

i) Poor intelligence

Research evidences reveal that visually impaired children have a poor I.Q. These researchers state that since the visually impaired children have considerable difficulties in the exploration of their environments, they have impairments in concept formation. It results in their poor performance in intelligence tests. On the contrary, recent western studies indicate that there is no reason to believe that blindness results in lower intelligence.

ii) Academic Retardation

Visually impaired children have poor academic achievements even if they use large-print books or Braille. They are noted to be retarded by at least one or two years and are found to be under-achievers. Visual impairment is the main factor for their slower acquisition of information. These children have a slower reading rate and lack concreteness in instructional procedures. Although the blind children and the low vision children are behind their sighted peers in academic achievement, their academic achievement is not affected as greatly as that of hearing impaired children.

iii) Slower Speech Development

Totally blind children can not learn the art of speech by imitation. They can only learn through what they hear and from occasional touch observation. Progress in speech development is not significant in comparison with their sighted peers due to the above reason. Research evidences indicate that acquisition of words may get hampered by blindness also. So these students should be provided with as rich an exposure to language as possible at as young an age as possible.

iv) Personality Disorders

It is a known fact that personality development includes both hereditary and environmental factors. It is a psychological organisation of the individuals modified by their life experiences. Congenitally blind children have life experiences, which are totally different from the life experiences of their sighted peers. These differences hamper their personality development to a considerable extent. Due to their impairment, the blind children are more likely to experience nervous strain and the feelings of insecurity and frustrations are common with them.

v) Problems in Social Adjustment

There is a great deal of conflicting evidence on whether visually impaired children are less well adjusted than their sighted peers. It is society's reaction to the blind person that determines the blind children's social adjustment or lack of it. When these children are looked down upon and ridiculed by sighted individuals, they feel inferior and this ultimately leads to maladjustment. Some research workers feel that visually impaired children are maladjusted in school but others refute it completely.

IDENTIFYING VISUALLY IMPAIRED CHILDREN

Early identification of visual impairment is indispensable so that correction can be provided at early stage itself before the problem becomes worse or complicated. Total blind can easily be recognised and identified but a detailed examination is necessary to identify low vision children. If the child has total blindness, it can be detected when the child is about one year old. But this is not possible with low vision children. The detection of low vision is a much more difficult proposition. Identification of visually impaired children is also associated with some behavioural symptoms. Teachers should watch for manifestation of these symptoms in the regular classrooms by any or some student(s). When they recognise such symptoms, they should subject the student(s) to medical examination.

SYMPTOMS THE CLASSROOM TEACHER SHOULD WATCH FOR BEHAVIOUR

- Rubs eye excessively
- Shuts or covers one eye, tilts head, or thrusts head forward
- Has difficulty in reading or in other work requiring close use of the eyes.
- Blinks more than usual or is irritable when doing close work.
- Holds books close to the eyes.
- Is unable to see distant things clearly
- Squints eyelids together or frowns.

Appearance

- Crossed eyes
- Red-rimmed, encrusted, or swollen eyelids
- Inflamed or watery eyes
- Recurring styles

Complaints

- Eyes itch, burn, or feel scratchy
- Can not see wall
- Dizziness, headaches, or nausea following close eye work
- Blurred or double vision

Methods to Identify Low Vision Children

Generally three methods are adopted to identify low vision children. They are:

i) Classroom observation,
ii) Ophthalmological examination, and
iii) Visual screening.

i) Classroom Observation

Any visual impairment in children can be detected by a careful classroom teacher by keen observation. The visually impaired children, especially the low vision children, are likely to exhibit certain behavioural symptoms. The classroom teacher can make use of the above furnished checklist to identify visual impairment on the basis of observation. Such students identified as visually impaired by means of classroom observation can be referred for medical examination and visual screening for confirmation of visual impairment and /or assessment of extent of impairment.

ii) Opthalmological Examination

The authentic method for identifying low vision children is opthalmological examination. By this method, children have to be medically examined before going to school. Low vision is assessed on the basis of visual acuity. Visual acuity is most often measured with the Snellen Chart, which consists of rows of letters for individuals who know the alphabet or Es for the very young and those who can not read. In the latter case, the Es are arranged in various positions, and the person is required to indicate in what position the "legs" of the Es are facing. Each row corresponds to the distance at which a person with normal vision can discriminate the direction of the Es.

There are eight rows, one corresponding to each of the following distances, 15,20,30,40,50,70,100 and 200 feet. People are normally tested at the 200-foot distance. If they can distinguish the direction of the letters in the 200 foot row, they are said to have 20 /20 central visual acuity for far distances. If they can distinguish only the much larger letters in the 70-foot row, they are said to have 20/70 central visual acuity for far distances. Thus those children who have visual acuity falling between 20/ 70 and 20/200 in the better eye with correction can be identified as low vision children.

iii) Visual Screening

There are screening procedures more thorough than the Snellen chart. Using these screening tests, teachers can identify children in need of a more complete eye examination. Unfortunately, some schools use only the Snellen chart as a screening procedure. But the Snellen chart does not pick up all possible types of visual problems. Visual screening may be undertaken by the District Health Officer also.

EDUCATION OF VISUALLY IMPAIRED CHILDREN

Lack of sight can severely limit a person's experiences because a primary means for obtaining information from the environment is not available. What makes the situation even more difficult is that educational experiences in the typical classroom are frequently visual. Nevertheless, most experts agree that we should educate visually, impaired students in the same general way as sighted children. Teachers need to make some modifications, but they can apply the same general educational principles. The important difference is that visually impaired students will have to rely on other sensory modalities to acquire information.

The students with little or no sight require special modifications in four major areas: (1) Braille, 92) use of remaining sight, (3) listening skills, and (4) mobility training. While the first three pertain to academic education, particularly reading, the last refers to skills needed for everyday living. Education should provide for smooth transitions from school life to social life.

BRAILLE

In nineteenth century France Louis Braille, who was himself blind, introduced the basic system of writing for the blind people that is used today. Braille based his alphabet on a system that had been developed by a French Officer, Charles Barber, for writing messages that could be read at night. The Braille method was offered as a replacement for raised line letters. In 1932, Standard English Braille was established as the standard code. As a result, all Braille readers could read, no matter who had trained them.

GRADES OF BRAILLE

The basic unit of Braille is a quadrangular cell. This cell contains anywhere from one to six dots. The different forms of Braille vary primarily in the number of contractions used. Grade 1 Braille, for example, contains no contractions. On the other hand, Grade 2 Braille makes considerable use of contractions and the shortened forms of words. Grade 1 Braille is easier to learn because it is more literal. But the Grade 2 Braille is the popular choice because it requires much less space and can be written and read much faster.

TWO MEANS OF WRITING IN BRAILLE

There are two means of writing in Braille. They are the Perkins Brailler and the slate and stylus.

The Perkins Brailler has six keys, one for each of the six dots of the cell. The key, when depressed simultaneously, leave an embossed print on the paper.

The slate and Stylus is more portable than the Perkins Brailler, but more difficult to use. The stylus must be pressed through the openings of the slate, which holds the paper between its two halves. The slate and stylus is also slower because the stylus makes an indentation in the paper, so the Braille cells have to be written in reverse order.

LIMITATIONS OF BRAILLE

A number of factors diminish the utility of reading Braille. First, it is difficult to learn, much more difficult than learning to read print. The contractions do not correspond to phonic rules. Also, reading Braille relies on memory to a great extent. As the perceptual unit is the single cell, readers have to perceive the matter much more sequentially. In addition to the above difficulty, they can not perceive a number of words at once, as can sighted persons reading print, Braille readers read much more slowly. Another factor that limits the utility of Braille is that the books are very large and take up a great deal of storage space. It is difficult to obtain reading material in Braille.

STATUS OF BRAILLE NOW

Because of Braille's limitations and because of advances in technology in other areas, fewer blind people rely on Braille than once was the case. Research surveys indicate that only about 15 percent of the blind population reads primarily by Braille. Thanks to a variety of technological devices, those who have little or no sight are turning more and more to auditory materials for their reading, and more and more low vision individuals are reading regular and large-print materials.

USE OF REMAINING SIGHT

There are many problems associated with reading Braille and the vast majority of visually impaired children have quite a bit of useful vision. So the teachers should encourage visually impaired children to use their sight as much as possible. The visually impaired children should read print because it ensures greater speed, the ability to portray pictures and diagrams and greater accessibility of reading materials.

TWO METHODS OF AIDING TO READ

There are two general methods of aiding visually impaired children to read print. They are large-print books and magnifying devices. Large-print books are simply books printed in large-size type. This text, printed primarily for sighted readers, is printed in 10-pcint type. Type sizes for visually impaired readers range upto 30-point type, but 18-point is one of the most popular. The major difficulty with large-type books is that a great deal of space is required to store them. Also, they are of limited availability.

Magnifying devices range from glasses and handhold lenses to closed-circuit television scanners that present enlarged images on a TV screen. These devices can be used with normal - size type or large-type books.

LISTENING SKILLS

Listening skill is very important for blind children. If the child is not able to rely on sight for gaining information from the environment, it is more crucial for him to become a good listener. It is wrong to assume that good listening skills will automatically develop in blind children. Research evidences indicate that blind children do not spontaneously compensate for poor vision by magically developing superior powers of concentration. In most cases, they must be taught how to listen. There are a variety of curriculum materials and programmes available to teach children listening skills.

The popularity of recorded material as a method of teaching visually impaired individuals has made listening skills more important. Visually impaired individuals now have access to records and tapes and a variety of recording devices. Use of recordings has distinct advantage over Braille or large-print books. The individual can cover the same material more quickly in a variety of ways. They can simply play the material at normal speed. This allows the individuals to "read" much faster than it would be possible with Braille. The most satisfactory method in terms of efficiency is to use a compressed speech device, which allows one to read at about 250 to 275, words per minute.

There are some disadvantages in using recordings. First, the student will come to rely too heavily on them and will not learn to use residual vision. Moreover, recordings are not available for everything. Listening to recordings requires a great deal of concentration. Any momentary lapse in attention will cause the student to miss what is being said.

MOBILITY TRAINING

How well individuals are able to cope with visual disability largely depends on how well they are able to move about. Whether a person withdraws from social environment or becomes independent depends greatly on mobility skills. There are four general methods available to aid visually impaired children in mobility. They are: (1) human guides, (2) guide dogs, (3) the long cane, and (4) electronic devices.

HUMAN GUIDES

The human guide provides the visually disabled person with greatest freedom in moving about safely, but this arrangement is not practical in most cases. Furthermore, too much reliance on another person causes a dependency that can be harmful. Most blind people who travel unaccompanied do not need help from those around them. Sometimes they may need verbal directions. If at all they need physical guidance, we should allow them to hold onto our arm above the elbow and walk a step behind us. We should not grasp the arm of blind individuals and "push" them in the direction they are heading.

GUIDE DOGS

Contrary to popular notions, a guide dog is also not recommended very often. Extensive training is required to teach the visually impaired person how to use a guide dog properly. The guide dogs are large and walk fast. So they are particularly inappropriate for children. Also, like any other pet they must be cared for. Another disadvantage is that the dog does not "take" the blind person anywhere. The blind person must first know where he or she is going; the dog is primarily a safeguard against walking into dangerous areas.

THE LONG CANE

Professionals most often recommend the long cane for those visually impaired individuals in need of a mobility aid. The long cane is the most effective and most efficient mobility aid yet devised for safe, independent travel by the majority of visually impaired people. The scanning system in which the user operates the cane provides echo-ranging cues and force-impact data that give vital information about immediate environment. It informs the user about the nature and condition of the surface underfoot, gives sufficient forewarning of down steps or drop-offs to prevent falls or injury, and protects the lower part of the body from collision.

The cane informs the user about various ground-surface textures, which can be related to specific areas and destinations. It allows investigation of the environment without actual hand contact. The long cane is reliable, long lasting and somewhat unaffected by unfavourable weather and temperature conditions. Although watching a skilled user of the long cane may give the impression that it is easy to manipulate, blind persons usually require extensive training in its proper use.

ELECTRONIC DEVICES

Researchers have developed quite a good number of sophisticated electronic devices for sensing of objects in the environment. Many of them are still experimental, most are quite expensive. The Laser cane and the sonicguide are good examples. These devices operate on the principle that human beings, like bats, can learn to locate objects by means of echoes.

The Laser cane has the advantage of being used in the same way as the long cane or as a sensing device that emits three beams of infrared light one up, one down, and one straight ahead. These are converted into sound after they strike objects in the path of the blind person.

The Sonic guide is still very much in the experimental stages. This ultrasonic aid may eventually help blind infants gain awareness of their spatial environment and objects within it. This device is worn on head. It emits ultrasound and converts reflections from objects into audible sound. On the basis of the characteristics of the sound, such as its pitch and clarity, and its direction, the sonic guide wearer can learn about such things as the distance, texture, and direction of objects in the environment. There are a number of unresolved issues relating to its use because the sonic guide is still experimental. So we have to keep in mind that electronic devices are:

1. Still experimental; we need to know a lot more about them.
2. Still very expensive; they are not available to everyone.
3. Not a substitute for more conventional techniques such as the long cane.
4. Not easily used; they require extensive training.
5. Not a substitute for spatial concepts; the blind person needs a fundamental sense of his or her spatial environment.

EDUCATION FOR TRANSITION

The very purpose of education for visually impaired adolescents is to ensure smooth transition from well-protected school life to highly competitive social life. Education for transition includes two closely related major areas-independence and employment. Blind people's major impediments to securing an appropriate job lie in the area of independent living.

INDEPENDENT LIVING

Visually impaired adolescents or adults constantly struggle to develop and maintain a sense of independence. It is a common mistake to assume that such an individual is helpless. This feeling is an outcome of our own experiences. When we enter a dark room for the first time, we feel defenceless, fearful. Visually impaired people, on the other hand, have had many opportunities to become accustomed to seeing little. So they are not at the same disadvantage as sighted people who suddenly find themselves in a situation in which there is little or no visibility.

In "The making of Blind men", Scott blames the dependency of blind people on the numerous organisations, agencies, and programmes created to serve them. He claims that blind people become dependent on the agencies for services and employment as they are taught to play a dependent role by these agencies. To promote independence in blind individuals the following suggestions should be adhered to.

1. Sighted people should not treat blind people in a stereotypical and demeaning manner for it will foster their dependency.
2. Sighted people should respect and encourage the blind person's individuality, capabilities and independence.
3. Blind people often do not need help. So the sighted people should not feel embarrassed or rejected if a blind person declines their offer of assistance.
4. Sighted people should try to avoid being over solicitous or overly protective. Blind people have the right to make mistakes, too.
5. Sighted people should feel free to approach and talk to a blind person. They can ask any question they wish. The blind person has the right to respond as he wishes.
6. When the sighted people leave the presence of a blind person, they should let him or her know that,
7. If sighted people have business with a blind person they should speak directly to the person rather than to sighted companions or relatives to get information.

If the sighted people adhere to the above suggestions, it will diminish the dependency of blind persons. Many things that sighted people can learn incidentally, we need to teach explicitly to visually impaired individuals, for example, how to work household appliances, eat at a table, or prepare food for cooking. It is the degree of their independent living that determines their success in employment.

EMPLOYMENT

Many working age blind adults are unemployed, and those who are working are often overqualified for the jobs they hold. Teachers should take an active role in helping visually impaired adolescents develop appropriate career aspirations, and job performance skills. Most authorities believe that although the emphasis on such preparation should be strongest in secondary school, it should begin in elementary school. Moreover, job training will be more likely to succeed if it is provided in regular work settings rather than in simulated settings in the classroom. The purpose of the training is not only to teach specific job tasks but also to give students a variety of real work experiences. In doing so, the students will be better prepared to make career decisions as adults. Besides, such an approach will provide the students with ample opportunities to develop generic work behaviours such as punctuality, grooming, following directions, and social skills, which will carry over to other work or community environment.

INSTRUCTIONAL MATERIALS

Children whose vision is severely impaired are usually diagnosed before they enter school, whereas the low vision students often are identified during vision screenings conducted in school. But these routine examinations are not foolproof. So the teacher has to employ observation technique. Teachers have many opportunities to observe children reading under a variety of conditions and to provide record of their observations by noting the symptoms of vision problems discussed in the identification section of this chapter.

Once the low vision children are identified in the general education classroom, the teacher should make use of special instructional materials to teach those visually impaired children in the general education classroom. The major difference between low vision children and blind children is their ability to read print. Students who have low vision can read print, although they may use magnifying glasses and require materials written in large print. On the other hand, blind children must be instructed by using Braille and aural methods, including records and audiotapes. Therefore, the visually impaired children in the mainstreamed classroom require adaptation of instructional materials. Although the itinerant or resource teacher will prepare or provide instructional materials written in Braille, it is the tape recording instructional lessons, assignments and tests that saves time and reduces the need for planning in advance. In addition, there are several organisations that provide audiotapes and records of a variety of textbooks and materials for pleasure reading.

In addition to adapted printed materials, there are a variety of other aids that visually impaired students can use in the general education classroom. Such aids are listed here categorywise.

A. Geography aids
   1. Braille atlases
   2. Moulded plastic relief maps
   3. Relief globes

B. Mathematical aids
   1. Abacus
   2. Raised clock faces
   3. Geometric area and volume aids
   4. Braille rulers
   5. Talking calculators

C. Writing aids
   1. Raised - line checkbooks
   2. Signature guides

D. Miscellaneous aids
   1. Audible goal locators, used as a goal, base, or object locator or a warning device.
   2. Braille or large type answer sheets.
   3. Science measurement kits including items such as thermometers, spring balances, gram weights.
   4. Sports - field kit including raised drawings of various sports' playing fields or courts.
   5. Simple machine kits including working models of pulleys, levers, plane, wheel, and axle.

Although students with low vision can read print, they also require adaptation of instructional material. They very much need modifications in written materials.

WRITTEN MATERIALS FOR LOW VISION CHILDREN

- Use purple dittoes as little as possible and then only when there is clear, sharp copy that has been typed in large print. Avoid hand-written dittoes.
- Use black ink on white paper or soft lead pencils and fiber-tipped, black ink pens on unglazed light and tinted paper, and use good quality typewriter ribbons to enhance the legibility of written materials.

- Arrange written materials on the page so that they are not crowded.
- Use only one side of the paper
- Outline dim areas of materials with a felt-tip pen.
- Select materials with non-gloss surfaces and high contrast.
- Write clearly in large print when preparing printed materials or when writing on the chalkboard.
- Keep chalkboards clean and write with a white chalk to enhance the contrast.
- Arrange for visually impaired children to sit in areas of high illumination when they are using duplicated materials.

TECHNOLOGICAL AND SPECIAL AIDS

The recent technological explosion has resulted in new electronic devices for the use of visually impaired individuals. Among them optacon occupies the foremost place.

Optacon is an electronic device very useful for visually impaired children for reading. The user of this device passes a hand-held scanner over printed material with one hand, and the visual letters are converted by pins into tactile letters on the index finger of the other hand. There is also an optacon II available that blind person can use to scan computer screens. These optacons are portable and also they make accessible many different kinds of materials, like magazines, newspapers, and computer screens. There are some disadvantages such as they are expensive and they allow slow rate of reading.

Kurzweil Reading Machine is another innovation, which has an advantage over the optacon in allowing a reading rate as fast as human speech. This small computer converts print into synthesised speech. The material is placed face down on a scanner and is "read" by an electronic voice. But this machine is so expensive that many institutions can not afford for it.

Versa Braille is another electronic device very useful for those who still wish to use Braille as a medium of instruction. Versa Braille saves time and space. The blind person records Braille onto tape cassettes and plays them back on the machine's reading board. A distinct advantage over traditional Braille is that the recorded material takes up much less space. There is also a versa Braille II plus, which can be used to convert letters on a personal computer screen into Braille.

Talking Calculator is an electronic device that can be effectively used for mathematics instruction. These devices "talk" to users by "saying" the numbers as they are punched and then "saying" the answer.

TEACHING VISUALLY IMPAIRED CHILDREN IN GENERAL EDUCATION CLASSROOM

Teachers have ample opportunities to observe students' reading under a variety of condition. They should keep a record of their observations by noting symptoms of vision problems. After recording the observations, the teacher may discuss the same with the person who conducts the vision screenings in school. He may discuss the vision problem of the particular student with the other teachers also. Then he should he decide upon the teaching techniques to try in his classroom.

TEACHING TECHNIQUES TO TRY

There are a few techniques which the general education classroom teacher can try in his classroom to teach visually impaired children. These techniques include adaptations of materials, instruction and classroom environment. A brief account of each adaptation is furnished below.

ADAPTATION OF EDUCATIONAL MATERIALS

The primary educational difference between students with low vision and students who are blind is their ability to read print. Students with low vision can read print though they may use magnifying classes and require materials written in large print. On the otherhand, blind students need materials written in Braille and aural methods including records and audiotapes. This warrants adaptation of instructional material for the mainstreamed visually impaired children. In addition to Braille, the teacher should make a maximum use of aural methods because recording of instructional lessons, assignments and tests saves time and reduces the need for planning far in advance. Also, several organisations have provided audiotapes and records of a variety of textbooks and materials for pleasure reading. Gearheart, Welshahn, and Gearheart (1988) have furnished a variety of other aids that the visually impaired children may find useful in classroom in addition to adapted printed materials.

A. Geography aids
1. Braille atlases
2. Moulded plastic relief maps
3. Relief globes

B. Mathematical Aids
1. abacus
2. raised clockfaces
3. geometric area and volume aids
4. Braille rulers
5. Talking calculators

C. Writing aids
1. raised line checkbooks
2. Signature guides

D. Miscellaneous aids
1. Audible goal locators, used as a goal, base, or object locator or a warning device.
2. Braille or large type answer sheets.
3. Science measurement kits (including such items as thermometers, spring balances, gram weights)
4. Sports field Kit (including raised drawings of various sports' playing fields or courts).
5. Simple machine kits(including working models of pulleys, levers, plane, wheel, and axle)

WRITTEN MATERIALS

Although the students with low vision can read print, they also need adaptations of educational materials. Harley and Lawrence (1984) recommend the following modifications.

- Use purple dittoes as little as possible and then only when there is clear, shop copy that has been typed in large print. Avoid hand written dittoes.
- Use black ink on white paper or soft lead pencils and fiber tipped, black ink pens on un glazed light and tinted paper, and use good quality typewriter ribbons to enhance the legibility of written materials.
- Arrange written materials on the page so that they are not crowded.
- Use only one side of the paper.
- Outline dim areas of the materials with a felt-tip pen.
- Select materials with mongloss surfaces and high contrast.
- Write clearly in large print when preparing printed materials or when writing on the chalkboard.
- Keep chalkboard clean and write with while chalk to enhance the contrast.
- Arrange for your visually impaired students to sit in areas of high illumination when they are using duplicated materials.

INSTRUCTIONAL ADAPTATIONS

Merely adapting educational materials also will not suffice. The classroom teacher has to make some modifications in the modes of instructions that will help the mainstreamed students. He can alternate activities that require close eye work with those that are less visually demanding. He can permit additional time for the blind and low vision children to complete reading assignments and to take tests. These will increase the likelihood of their success in general education classroom. Further, the teacher should use concrete materials and hands-on to improve the instruction of visually impaired students, who often do not have the same background and experiences as their nondisabled classmates. Also, the teacher should repeat information as he writes on the chalkboard aloud and allow the students to examine closely demonstrations presented by him and other students in the class.

ADAPTATIONS IN THE CLASSROOM ENVIRONMENT

Visually impaired students require orientation to the physical arrangement of the room, including the location of materials, desks, activity areas, and the teacher's desk, and exits. So the teacher can orient the students with visual impairment more rapidly to familiarise them with these features from one focal point, such as their desk. Once the students are oriented to the classroom, efforts may be taken to make them familiar with the school and surrounding grounds, learning the location of gym, library restrooms, cafeteria, water fountains and playground. Whenever there are changes in and additions to the classroom or school arrangements, the visually impaired students must be informed of the same. Normally, visually impaired students must be encouraged to move about without the aid of sighted guides. However, when there are special events and activities that take place outside the classroom such as fire drills and assemblies, the teacher may assign a sighted.

Appropriate seating in the class is very important for it will improve their visual opportunities. The teacher many allow the students with low vision to change their seats whenever they need more or less light. This will eliminate many difficulties. They may be allowed to sit close to the chalkboard. Students with visual impairment deserve the same instruction in all content areas as their nondisabled classmates. However, it is very necessary to provide the visually impaired students with special instruction in skill areas required to meet their specific needs, such as social, sensory motor, independent, daily living and mobility training. These should be taken care of by professionals and the classroom teacher must be aware of them.

SUMMARY

Like anyone with a disability, the behind children want to be treated like everyone else. Most blind children do not seek pity or even unnecessary help. Although they may require assistance in some situations, mostly they prefer to be reminded of their similarities rather than differences.

There are two ways of describing visual impairment. One is legal definition and the other educational definition. According to legal classification system a person is said to be legally blind if he has visual acuity of 20/200 or less in the better eye even with connection or has a field of vision so narrow that its widest diameter subtends an angular distance no greater than 20 degrees. Partially sighted individuals are those who have visual acuity falling between 20/70 and 20/200 in the better eye with correction.

For educational purpose blind children are those whose vision is so severely impaired that they must learn to read Braille or use aural methods such as audiotapes and records. Those visually impaired children who can read print, even if they need magnifying glasses or large print books are referred to as having low vision.

Errors of refraction, glaucoma, cataraets, and diabetes, prenatal causes, improper muscle functioning are some of the major causes of visual impairment.

The psychological and behaviour characteristics of visually impaired children include restricted language development, lag in conceptual development, tactual perception, obstacle sense, difficulty in social skills and stereotypic behaviours.

Poor intelligence, academic retardation, slower speech development, personality disorders, problems in social adjustment, are some of the problems encountered by the visually impaired children in educational process.

A classroom teacher can identify visually impaired children by means of classroom observation, opthalmological examination and visual screening.

Educational programmes for visually impaired children include use of Braille, use of remaining sight and mobility training. To teach visually impaired children in general education classrooms the teacher should make adaptations in the instruction, instructional materials and in the classroom environment.

REFERENCE

Chintamani Kar (1992) *Exceptional Children: Their Psychology and Instruction*. Sterling Publishers, New Delhi.

Gearheart, B.R., Welshahn, M.W., and Gear heart, C.J. (1988) *The Exceptional Student in the Regular Classroom.* Chas E. Merill, Columbus, OH.

Hallahan, D.P, and Kauffman, J.M. (1991) *Exceptional Children: Introduction to Special Education.* Prentice Hall International Limited, London.

Harley, R.K. and Lawrence, G.A. (1984) *Visual Impairments in the Schools.* Chas C. Thomas, Springfield, IL.

Jangira, N.K. and others (1988) *Source Book for Teaching Visually Disabled Children.* NCERT, New Delhi.

Scott, R.A (1969) *The Making of Blind Men.* Russell Sage Foundation, New York.

3

SPEECH AND HEARING IMPAIRED CHILDREN

OBJECTIVES

This chapter deals with nature, causes and categories of speech and hearing impairments. Also, it outlines the educational provision for these impaired children. After reading this chapter, the readers should be able to:

1. Define speech and hearing impairments.
2. Understand the causative factors of speech and hearing impairments.
3. Classify speech and hearing impaired children.
4. Identify speech and hearing impaired children.
5. Develop an insight into the educational provisions of these impaired children.
6. Understand the role of sophisticated technology in the education of speech and hearing impaired children.

Communication is such a natural part of our everyday lives that we usually do not think about it. Speech and language are tools used for purposes of communication. Communication requires encoding (sending in understandable form) and recording (receiving and understanding) messages. Communication involves a sender and receiver of messages, but it does not always involve language. For example, animals communicate through movements and noises. We are concerned with communication through language.

Social conversations with family, friends, relatives, and casual acquaintances are normally so effortless and pleasant that it is hard to imagine anyone having difficulty with it. On the other hand, most people have feelings of inadequacy of their speech or language only in stressful or unusual social situation.

DEFINITION

Speech is the behaviour of forming and sequencing the sounds of oral language. It is the most common symbol system used in communication between human beings. Speech disorders are impairments in the production and use of oral language. They include disabilities in producing voice, making speech sounds (articulation), and producing speech with a normal flow (fluency). When the speech of a person differs significantly from others to the extent of calling attention to itself or interfering with communication, it is diagnosed as a speech defect. The number of children suffering from speech defects is much more than that from any type of impairment.

Children with communication disorders are not receiving an appropriate amount of services from speech language pathologists and audiologists. There is a need for more speech language pathologists in the schools, as well as greater knowledge of communication disorders by special and general education teachers and greater involvement of teachers in helping students learn to communicate effectively.

SPEECH DISORDERS

Speech disorders can be classified on the basis of etiology according to which it may be organic or functional. Organic group includes speech disorders caused by palatal anomalies, dental irregularities, paralysis and tumours of the larynx, brain damage etc. Functional group represents failure to learn speech due to general personality and emotional disturbances. But this dichotomy is not crystal clear. Some authorities think that the classification of speech disorders depends mainly on the purpose of classification. It may be classified according to the major symptoms, such as voice disorders, articulation disorders, delayed speech, fluency disorder. An individual may have more than one disorder of speech and speech and language disorders sometime occur together.

VOICE DISORDERS

People's voices are perceived as having pitch, loudness, and quality. Changes in pitch and loudness are part of the stress patterns of speech. Vocal quality is not only related to production of speech sounds but also to the non-linguistic aspects of speech. Together, the three dimensions of voice are sufficient to reveal a person's identity. It is very difficult to precisely define voice disorders. Voice disorders are characteristics of pitch, loudness, and /or quality that are abusive of the larynx and hamper communication. Voice disorders are perceived as markedly different from what is customary for someone of a given age, sex, and cultural background.

Disorders of phonation are voice disorders that involve a dysfunction within the larynx.

Disorders of resonance are voice disorders that involve the dysfunction of the oral and nasal air passageways

ARTICULATION DISORDERS

Distinctions between articulation disorders are sometimes difficult to make. *Phonology* refers to the study of the rules for using the sounds of language. When a person has difficulty in communicating because he or she does not use speech sounds according to standard rules, the disorder, is phonological. Articulation refers to the movements of the articulators in production of the speech sounds that make up words of our language.

Articulation and phonological disorders involve errors in producing words. Word sounds may be omitted, substituted, disordered or added. Missing, substituted, added, or poorly produced word sounds may make a speaker difficult to understand or even unintelligible. Such errors in speech production subject the speaker to teasing or ridicule.

FLUENCY DISORDERS

Normal speech is characterised by some interruptions in speech flow. All of us occasionally get speech sounds in the wrong order (revalent for relevant), speak too fast to be understood, pause at the wrong place in a sentence, use an inappropriate pattern of stress, or become disfluent. We stumble, backtrack, repeating syllables or words, and fill in pauses with "uh" while trying to think of how to finish what we have to say. Students with fluency disorders take intensive effort to speak. Frequency of interruptions in their flow of speech is so high that it keeps them from being understood or draws extraordinary attention.

The most frequent type of fluency disorder is stuttering. About 1 percent of children and adults are stutterers. More boys than girls stutter. Most stutterers can be identified by at least age five. But parents can perceive their child as stuttering as early as twenty to thirty months of age. Most of the stutterers begin to show an abnormal speech pattern between two and five years of age. Many children outgrow their childhood disfluencies.

DELAYED SPEECH

Statistics reveal that this disorder occurs with greater frequency than any other communication disorder. Different studies report that the sole cause of delayed speech is hearing loss, mental retardation, cerebral dysfunction, emotional disturbances and environmental deprivation. Very often, children do not speak at the usual age due to lack of motivation. Of course, there are many causes of delayed speech and the diagnosis and treatment involve services from a number of professionals. Given proper training, the children with delayed speech can develop their ability to speak well and will be able to speak as fluently as others before they become adults.

CAUSES OF SPEECH DISORDERS

There are various causes of speech impairment. Some important causes are discussed below.

i) Organic Causes

Palatal anomalies, dental irregularities, paralysis and tumours of the larynx, brain damage are some of the organic causes of speech disorders. In some cases, deformation of jaw and lips also result in lisping. Cleft-palate causes voice and articulation disorders.

ii) Functional Causes

Although some children have normal speech mechanisms, they have disorders in articulation and voice. Imitation of an older sibling, a playmate, or an adult may be the sole cause for this type of anomaly. It is to be noted that children usually learn to articulate, vocalise and use language "by ear". They learn to speak in such manner as they hear. Therefore, speech disorders are based on imitation of adult's behaviour.

iii) Psychogenic Causes

Recent research studies indicate that many speech disorders are psychogenic. When the causes of speech disorders are not organic or functional, they can be attributed to the children's reactions to the environment they live in, particularly their parents. Functional articulatory disorders of children are definitely and significantly associated with maladjustment and undesirable traits on the part of the parents.

iv) Psychological Causes

Speech disorders can be ascribed to emotional and psychological origin also. The efficacy of the speech organs alone can not guarantee good speech. Good speech depends on the personal maturity of the child, his attitude to himself, his relationship with others, and the degree to which the home has stimulated and encouraged speech. Some authorities observe that speech disorders are the outcome of disturbed feeling or emotions, faulty language habits arising from social pressures.

v) Loss of Hearing

Normal auditory system is very essential for development of speech reception skill. If the child has hearing impairment, the auditory input will be distorted. This will result in deviation or delay in development of speech reception skills. This faulty feedback system will affect speech production. Research findings indicate that the degree of hearing loss has a direct bearing on the production of speech and language.

vi) Social Influences

Language is a means of communication. Social environment is essential for development of language skills. If the environment is impoverished, children may not get due stimulation. They may not get adequate opportunities to learn new words. Stimulating homes, schools, and peer group play a pivotal role in the language acquisition and achievement of children. That is why children from higher professional groups evince early speech development.

vii) Cerebral palsy

Children who are victims of cerebral palsy often lack stimulation to speak. Therefore, they should be highly motivated for speech therapy. Spastics, athetoid and ataxic children often have a good number of speech disorders. Spastic child evinces articulatory deviation and athetoid child shows slurring in rhythm and constant change in pitch.

EDUCATION FOR SPEECH IMPAIRED CHILDREN

Helping children overcome speech and language disorders is not the responsibility of a single profession. Identification is the joint responsibility of the classroom teacher, the speech-language pathologist, and the parents. By listening attentively and empathetically when children speak, providing appropriate models of speech and language for children to imitate, and encouraging children to use their communication skills appropriately, the classroom teacher can help not only to improve speech and language but also to prevent disorders from developing in the first place.

ROLE OF THE TEACHER

Teachers play a pivotal role in the speech development of students. By virtue of their position and everyday observation the teachers can easily observe any deviation in the speech of their children. Early identification is very important to provide prompt remediation or correction. There are certain symptoms or indicators, which are, associated with specific speech disorders. An insight into these symptoms is essential for the teacher to devise or plan appropriate remediation or correction. Some of these indicators are discussed below.

Indicators of Articulation disorders

1. Omission of certain sounds from speech (e.g. ca for car)
2. Substitution of certain sounds for other sounds (e.g. wabbit for rabbit)
3. Reversal of order of sounds within words (e.g. aminal for animal)
4. Difficulty in saying certain speech sounds(e.g. sh/r/th)
5. Frequent non speech vocalisations (e.g. clicks tongue, hums)
6. Difficulty in performing oral movements (e.g. chewing, yawning, sticking out tongue)

Indicators of Fluency and Voice Disorders

1. Constant congestion or nasality
2. Constantly harsh-sounding or breathy-sounding voice
3. Continual hoarseness
4. Speaking in a too-soft voice
5. Speaking in a sing-song voice
6. Speaking in monotone
7. Speaking too slowly or too fast
8. Unusually high or low voice pitch
9. Unusual pattern of stressing words in sentences
10. Struggling to say words (e.g. grimaces, blinks eyes, clenches fists)

After identifying speech-impaired children, the teacher should ensure the following educational provisions.

i) Speech Therapy

When a child is in need of speech or language therapy, he should be referred to an expert or a therapist for consultation. Very often, there may not be any facility in schools for this purpose. If it is so, the parents should be instructed to take the child to the nearest speech or hearing centre. Generally the speech therapists help children in correcting and removing the disorders in articulation. They take effort to minimize stuttering as far as practicable. For treatment of stammering psychotherapists must be consulted, not the speech therapists. It is because some psychological factors are responsible for stammering.

ii) Articulation Correction

Owing to various reasons, the parents are, very often, not in a position to obtain the required help for their children. Under such circumstances, the resource teacher can help the children in the school itself when he has time to spare. The teacher can try to make simple corrections of articulation disorders. If the teacher possesses good articulation and modulation, he will be able to make a good impact on children. He can enable his children to circumvent their deficiency to a considerable extent

iii) Speech Training Activities

Teaching experts can make an impressive contribution by providing the children with practice in using the correct sound after it has been successfully elicited by the speech therapists. Speech training activities must be provided taking groups into consideration. Activities such as rhymes, jingles, and speech games will be very useful in speech training activities.

iv) Extra Curricular Activities

In addition to the above activities, these children should be taken to visit places of interest such as historical, social, cultural, or geographical places. It may be museums, factories, workshops, dams or lakes, animal zoo etc. where they will get adequate opportunities and stimulation to gather new experiences. The interactions the students will have in such places will help them learn many new words. As a result, they will develop their active vocabulary and will be encouraged to embark on new ventures like reading books, journals, magazines etc.

v) Cooperative Learning

To assist students with speech and language disorders cooperative learning is of much value. It facilitates learning and maximises communication. In cooperative learning, students work together in small groups to reach a common goal. They are accountable not only for their own achievement but also for the learning of other group members. This interdependence makes cooperative learning an effective technique to integrate students with disabilities into mainstream classes because it promotes learning, communication, and positive attitudes among diverse students. Cooperative learning can be used effectively to circumvent the speech disorders of speech impaired children.

HEARING IMPAIRED CHILDREN

Hearing is the main sensory pathway through which speech and verbal communication develop. If a child hears imperfectly, he is likely to speak incorrectly. Again, hearing also influences learning and other aspects of maturation. Early detection of hearing impairment is very important for the child's over-all development. A defect in hearing mechanism will result in perceptual problems. Hearing impairment adversely affects our knowledge of the world around us. Further, it also hampers the child's performance in learning. Hearing-impaired children are more disadvantaged than visually impaired children. Hearing impairment is a greater barrier to the normal development of language.

DEFINITION OF HEARING IMPAIRMENT

There are many definitions and classification systems of hearing impairment. By far the most common division is between deaf and hard of hearing. These two categories are defined differently by different professionals. The extreme points of view are represented by clinicians and educators. Those who maintain physiological viewpoint are interested primarily in the measurable degree of hearing loss. Children who can not hear sounds at or above a certain intensity (loudness) level are classified as deaf; others with a hearing loss are classified as hard of hearing. Hearing sensitivity is measured in terms of decibels. Decibels are units of relative loudness of sounds. Zero decibels (O dB) designate the point at which people with normal hearing can detect the faintest sound. Each succeeding number of decibels denotes a certain degree of hearing loss. Those who maintain physiological viewpoint consider those children with hearing losses of about 90 dB or greater to be deaf and those with hearing losses below 90 db to be hard of hearing.

But educators do not maintain this viewpoint. They are concerned with how much the hearing loss is likely to affect the child's ability to speak and develop language. Because of the close causal link between hearing loss and delay in language development, educators categorise on the basis of spoken language abilities. Following are the most commonly accepted set of definitions reflecting this educational orientation.

Hearing Impairment is a generic term indicating a hearing disability, which may range in severity from mild to profound; it includes the subsets of deaf and hard of hearing.

A Deaf Person is one whose hearing disability precludes successful processing of linguistic information through audition, with or without a hearing aid.

A Hard of Hearing Person is one who, generally with the use of hearing aid, has residual hearing sufficient to enable successful processing of linguistic information through audition.

TYPES OF HEARING IMPAIRMENT

The age of onset of hearing impairment and the relationship between hearing loss and language delay are important considerations in the classification of hearing impaired children. The earlier the hearing loss manifests itself in a child's life, the more difficulty he or she will have in developing language. For this reason, professionals classify hearing impaired children as follows.

Congenitally deaf are those children who are born deaf.

Adventitiously deaf are those children who acquire deafness at some time after birth.

There are two other frequently used terms, which are more specific in pinpointing language acquisition as critical.

Prelingual deafness is deafness present at birth, or occurring early in life at an age prior to the development of speech or language.

Postlingual deafness is deafness occurring at any age following the development of speech or language. Experts differ regarding the dividing point between prelingual and postlingual deafness. Some believe it should be at about eighteen months, whereas others think it should be lower, at about twelve months or even six months.

The following classification system is also common. This classification is based on hearing sensitivity.

Mild deaf are those children who have hearing losses between 26 and 54 decibels.

Moderate deaf are those children who have hearing losses between 55 and 69 decibels.

Severe deaf are those children who have hearing losses between 70 and 89 decibels.

Profound deaf are those children who have hearing losses of about 90 decibels or greater.

Some authorities object that any of the various classification systems should not be followed strictly. These definitions are not precise because they deal with events that are difficult to measure and that occur in variable organisms. So we should not form any hard-and-fast opinions about an individual's ability to hear and speak solely on the basis of a classification system.

CHARACTERISTICS OF HEARING IMPAIRED CHILDREN

Hearing impaired children have certain distinct psychological and behavioural characteristics. The nature and severity of certain limitation pertaining to hearing impaired children cause certain changes in behaviour. The following are some important characteristics of hearing impaired individuals.

i) Linguistic Difficulties

Hearing impaired babies babble less than hearing infants by as early as eight months of age, or even earlier. The babbling they make is also of a qualitatively different nature. These differences occur because hearing infants are reinforced by hearing their own babbling and by hearing the verbal responses of adults. Deaf are unable to hear either themselves or others, so they are not reinforced. The lack of feedback is another cause for deaf children's poor speech production. Moreover, deaf children hear and imitate, so they are deprived of an adequate adult model. Owing to the above reason, the hearing impaired children are abnormally slow in their linguistic development.

These children have a limited vocabulary, they lack comprehension of complex words and words with multiple meaning and concept.

ii) Problems in Personal and Social Development

Social and personality development depends heavily on communication. Social interaction is the communication of ideas between two or more people. Because of society's heavy dependence on language, hearing impaired individuals have personality and social characteristics that are different from those of people with normal hearing ability. As the hearing impaired children are frequently cut off from communicating with the population at large, they grow up in relative isolation. They experience considerable difficulty in making friends. They are often perceived as excessively shy. This tendency toward withdrawn behaviour will be more pronounced if they do not have hearing impaired parents or peers with whom they can interact nonverbally. Hard of hearing and, especially, deaf children tend, more than any other handicapped group to mix socially with people who have the same handicap.

iii) Personality Problems

Research evidences indicate that hearing impaired children face personality problems. Partially deaf children experience more confrontation and personality problems than the totally deaf children. It is because partially deaf children get more frustrated as they try to reach the level of the normal children whereas of totally deaf children seem reconciled to their fate.

iv) Psychological Characteristics

Whether hearing impaired will develop behavioural problems depends on how well those in the children's environment accept the disability. Hence, family climate is critical in determining the behavioural problem of the hearing impaired children. Children develop inferiority complex because of their inability to adapt to circumstances that require verbal communication. They always compare themselves with their normal peers and judge the attitudes of the society towards them. They feel that the attitude of the society towards them is not normal. They view it as either overprotective or rejective. They feel that they are very different from normal children. This feeling hampers their growth and development of personality.

v) Abnormal Emotional Behaviour

Young hearing impaired children evince abnormal emotional behaviour. They may throw tantrums to attract the attention to themselves or their deeds or needs. Lack of comprehension causes tension and resistance. They are frequently obstinate and have tendency to tease. They become irritated when they find it very difficult to make them understood. Recently, some authorities argue that severe emotional disturbance is no more prevalent in deaf individuals than in those with hearing.

CAUSES OF HEARING IMPAIRMENT

Some authorities categorise the causes of hearing impairment under four headings: (I) hereditary and non-hereditary, (ii) congenital and acquired, (iii) prenatal, perinatal, and postnatal, and (iv) physiological and psychological. But, in this text, causes of hearing loss are classified on the basis of the location of the problem within the hearing mechanism.

CONDUCTIVE, SENSORINEURAL, AND MIXED IMPAIRMENTS

There are three major classifications of causes of hearing loss on the basis of the location of the problem within the hearing mechanism. They are conductive hearing losses, sensorineural hearing losses, and mixed hearing losses.

A conducted loss refers to impairments that interfere with the transfer of sound along the conductive pathway of the ear. Anatomically, conductive losses are the result of problems of the outer and /or middle ear.

Sensorineural impairments involve problems confined to the inner ear. In this case, the sound is conducted properly and the difficulty lies in analysing or perceiving it properly. There is no surgical remedy for this malady. Hearing aids for amplification of sound has little to do with this impairment

Mixed impairments refer to a combination of the first two impairments

IMPAIRMENTS OF THE OUTER EAR

The auricle and external auditory canal of the outer ear are less important than the middle and inner ear for hearing. However, several conditions of the outer ear, particularly the external auditory canal, can cause the child to be hard of hearing. The presence of foreign objects in the external ear causes hearing loss. Tumours of the external auditory canal, if large enough, are another source of impairment. Excessive build up of cerumen, or earwax, can result in hearing problems. Finally, perforation of the eardrum, which may result from any of a number of causes, ranging from blow to the head to excessive pressure in the middle ear, can also produce hearing impairment.

IMPAIRMENTS OF THE MIDDLE EAR

Abnormalities of the middle ear cause hearing losses and these losses are generally more serious than those of the external ear. But middle ear problems do not result in deafness. Children with impairments arising from middle ear problems are usually classified as heard of hearing. Most of the middle ear problems are correctable with medical or surgical treatment. Most middle ear hearing losses occur because the mechanical action of the assicles is interfered with in some way.

Otitis media is an infection of the middle ear space and it is the most common problem of the middle ear. Although otitis media can affect individuals of any age, it is primarily a disease of childhood, occurring most commonly in children under the age of two years. It can cause temporary conductive hearing loss. If it is not treated properly, it can eventually lead to rupture of the tympanic membrane.

Non-supportive otitis media is also a middle ear problem of some significance. This condition can occur even without infection. It usually results from a disruption of the functioning of the Eustachian table such that negative pressure occurs in the middle ear. It causes the blood serum of the middle ear lining to be sucked into the middle ear cavity. Thus it causes hearing impairment.

Otosclerosis is a disease of the bone that causes the stages to become abnormally attached to the oval window. Although it rarely occurs in children, it causes hearing impairment when it afflicts an individual.

IMPAIRMENTS OF THE INNER EAR

The most severe hearing impairments are associated with the inner ear. Inner ear hearing losses present the greatest problems for both educators and clinicians. Causes of inner ear disorders can be hereditary or acquired. The most frequent cause of childhood deafness is heredity. Acquired hearing losses of the inner ear include those due to bacterial infections, pre-maturity, viral infections, prenatal infections of the mother, unwanted side effects of some antibiotics, and excessive noise levels. There is a relationship between the cause of the hearing impairment and the degree of hearing loss. The most devastating losses occur due to bacterial infections such as meningitis, prenatal infections of mother such as rubella, and hereditary factors.

IDENTIFYING HEARING IMPAIRED CHILDREN

The teachers can use systematic observation and then specific hearing tests to identify the hearing impaired individuals. Recent advancement in technology has made the identification procedure easier. The following are some important techniques for identifying hearing impaired children.

i) Systematic Observation

This method is highly conducive and extremely useful for identifying hearing impaired individuals. There are certain observable points of behaviour pertaining to hearing impaired individuals, which form the base for teachers' initial identification. Some such behaviours are:

- They turn heads on one side to hear better.
- These children are unable to follow directions.
- In the classroom, they always request the teacher to repeat instructions, questions etc.,
- They focus specially on the speaker's lips.
- They always hesitate to participate in group discussions.
- They display restlessness, inattention and speech difficulty.
- Frequent ear eggs are observable.

ii) Case Study

Psychiatrists usually adapt this technique. They collect data directly from the child or from a close relative of the child. While collecting date, the following points must be taken into account.

- Identification of the child, i.e. name, address, etc.
- Statement of the present problem (symptoms etc).
- Health history (illness, serious disease, surgical operation etc.).
- Developmental history.

iii) Hearing Tests

There are three different types of hearing tests: pure-tone audiometry, speech audiometry, and specialised tests for very young children. Depending on the characteristics of the examinee and the use to which the results will be applied, the audiologist may choose to give any number of tests from any one or a combination of these three categories.

a) Pure-Tone Audiometry

Pure-tone audiometry is designed to establish the individual's capacity for hearing at a variety of different frequencies. A person's threshold for hearing is simply the level at which he or she can first detect a sound. It refers to how intense a sound must be before the person can detect it. Intensity of sound is measured in units known as decibels (dB).

Pure-tone audiometers present tones of various intensities (dB levels) at various frequencies (HZ). Frequency is measured in units known as Hertz (HZ). It refers to the number of vibrations per unit of time of a sound wave; the pitch is higher with more vibrations, lower with fewer. Hertz are usually measured from 125 Hz (low sounds) to 8000 Hz (high sounds). Sounds below 125 Hz and above 8000 Hz are not measured because most speech does not fall within this range.

The procedure for testing a person's sensitivity to pure tones is relatively simple. Each ear is tested separately. The audiologist presents a variety of tones within the range of 0 to about 110 dB and 125 to 8000 Hz until he or she establishes at what level of intensity (dB) the individual can detect the tone of a number of frequencies - 124 Hz, 250 Hz, 500Hz, 1000Hz, 2000Hz, 4000 Hz, and 8000 Hz. For each of these frequencies there is a measure of degree of impairment. A 50dB hearing loss at 500 Hz, for example, means the person is able to detect the 500 Hz sound when it is given at an intensity level of 50dB, whereas the normal person would have heard it at 0 dB.

b) Speech Audiometry

The ability to detect and understand speech is of prime importance. So a technique called speech audiometry has been developed to test a person's detection and understanding of speech. Speech detection is defined as the lowest level (in dB) at which the individual can detect speech without understanding. But the dB level at which one can understand speech is more important. This is known as the speech reception threshold (SRT). To measure SRT the person must be provided with a list of two-syllable words, testing each ear separately. The dB level at which he or she can understand half of the words is often used as an estimate of SRT level.

c) Specialised Test for very Young Children

A basic assumption for pure-tone and speech audiometry is that the persons being treated understand what is expected of them. None of these will be effective for very young children under about four years of age or for children with other handicaps.

Play Audiometry

This technique is used to establish rapport with the children and to motivate them to respond. The examiner sets up the testing situation as a game. Using pure tones or speech, the examiner teaches the children to do various activities whenever they hear a signal. The activities are designed to be attractive for young children. For example, children may be acquired to pick up a block, square a toy, or open a book.

REFLEX AUDIOMETRY

Children normally possess some reflexive behaviours to loud sounds, which are useful for the testing of hearing by reflex audiometry. More reflex is present at birth. It is defined as a movement of the face, body, arms, and legs and blinking of the eyes. Another response that may be used to determine hearing ability is the orienting response. This response is evident when the children turn their head and body towards the source of sound.

EVOKED RESPONSE AUDIOMETRY

Evoked response audiometry is a method of measuring hearing in a person unable to make voluntary responses. In this technique, changes in brain-wave activity are measured by using an electroencephalograph (EEG). Sounds heard by an individual are converted into electrical signals within the brain. This method has become very popular with the advent of sophisticated computers. Evoked-response audiometry is very expensive and difficult to interpret. But it has certain advantages. This can be used during sleep even without the awareness of children.

iv) School Screening

It is easy to identify children with severe hearing losses but it is not so easy to identify children with mild hearing losses. For that some routine screening procedures are necessary. Screening tests can be administered either individually or in a group. In group setting the examiner presents pure tones to children one at a time or to more than one child at a time. Each child has a pair of earphones and is instructed to keep his or her eyes closed and to raise his or her hand upon hearing a tone.

EDUCATION FOR HEARING IMPAIRED CHILDREN

The problem that plagues every educator of children with hearing impairment is how to communicate with their students. Also, teaching them how to communicate with others is also a formidable task. There are two approaches to teach communication to hearing impaired children. They are:

i) Oral approach, and
ii) Total Communication approach

i) Oral Approach

Oral approach advocates teaching deaf people to speak. It is different from manualism, which advocates use of some kind of manual communication. Manualism was popular and very much preferred until the middle of the nineteenth century when oralism began to gain predominance. Currently most educators advocate the use of both oral and manual methods. It is known as total communication approach. Oral approach includes auditory training and speech reading.

AUDITORY TRAINING

Auditory training is the procedure of teaching the deaf and hard of hearing children to make use of what hearing they possess. Advocates of this approach claim that all but a very few totally deaf children are able to benefit from auditory training. The recent technological advances in the development of hearing aid have augmented the benefit of auditory training. Auditory training involves three major goals. They are:

1. Development of awareness of sound
2. Development of the ability to make gross discriminations among environmental sounds.

3. Development of the ability to discriminate among speech sounds.

DEVELOPMENT OF AWARENESS OF SOUND

The first task in auditory training is to ascertain that the child knows that there are a variety of sounds, including speech, in the environment. Those children who have not used hearing aids since early infancy may experience some difficulty in adjusting to them. The sounds they hear for the first time may sound so overwhelming that they learn to "tune them out". So the advocates of auditory training stress the importance of introducing hearing aids as early as possible.

GROSS DISCRIMINATION OF ENVIRONMENTAL SOUNDS

Once the child develops awareness of sound, the teachers should begin the process of teaching gross discrimination of environmental sounds. This training sometimes requires children to match prerecorded environmental sounds with their corresponding pictures.

DISCRIMINATION AMONG SPEECH SOUNDS

Discrimination of speech sounds requires much more sophisticated learning on the part of the children than does the discrimination of gross environmental sounds. One of the reasons for speech discrimination training being so complicated is that everyday speech often occurs among a variety of factors, referred to as "noise", which can reduce the discriminality of speech sounds. Speech discrimination training in the early stages should take place under ideal, low noise conditions. But the children must gradually learn to cope with discriminating speech under more natural conditions, which are relatively high in noise.

SPEECHREADING

Speechreading is sometimes inappropriately called lipsreading. It involves teaching hearing impaired children how to use visual information to understand what is being said to them. Speechreading is a more accurate term than lipsreading because the latter refers only to the use of visual cues arising from movement of the mouth in speaking. It does not take into account the other visual stimuli in the environment, which can help the hearing impaired persons to understand spoken language. On the other hand, speechreading makes an effective use of visual information. There are three general kinds of visual information that speechreaders can try to take advantage of. They are:

1. Stimuli from the environment.
2. Stimuli associated with the message but not part of speech.
3. Stimuli directly connected with the production of speech.

ENVIRONMENTAL STIMULI

Speech reading depends greatly on the ability to pay attention to and obtain meaning from the environment. Good speech readers are able to anticipate certain kinds of messages in certain situations.

NONVERBAL STIMULI RELATED TO THE SPEAKERS

Training in this area involves teaching the children that some actions of the speaker are more likely to be connected with certain messages. Facial expressions are a very good example. For instance, a person talking about a serious accident would not be smiling.

Speech Stimuli, the most important aspect of speechreading, is the ability to discriminate among the various speech sounds by relying on visual cues from the lips, tongue, and jaw. For example, to learn to discriminate among vowels, the speech reader concentrates on cues related to the degree of jaw opening and lip shaping.

LIMITATIONS OF SPEECHREADING

Unfortunately, speechreading is extremely difficult, and good speechreaders are rare. There are many factors that make speechreading so hard. For one thing, many sounds are produced with little obvious movement of the mouth.

- Also, they find the homophones very difficult to discriminate.
- They can not distinguish among the pronunciation of (p), (b), or (m).
- There is a great variability among speakers in how they visibly produce sounds.

ii) Total Communication Approach

Two factors played pivotal role for the shift that occurred in the 1970s from oral-only instruction to total communication, the use of oral and manual methods. The factors are:

1. A number research studies found that deaf children of deaf parents who had been exposed to manual methods, when compared to deaf children of hearing parents who had not been so exposed, were superior in English skills, academic achievement, writing, reading, and social maturity. In addition, there were no differences in speech between the two groups.
2. There was a growing dissatisfaction with the effectiveness of oral-only methods, particularly at the preschool level.

These two factors led to a new approach, known as total communication approach, which makes use of both oral and manual methods. About two-thirds of all deaf children are now taught by total communication approach and one-third are taught by an oral approach.

SIGNING ENGLISH SYSTEMS

Signing English systems are the type of manualism most often used in the total communication approach.

Fingerspelling is the representation of letters of the English alphabet by finger positions. It is also used occasionally to spell out certain words, such as proper nouns.

Singing English Systems refer to signing systems that have been devised for the express purpose of teaching deaf children to communicate.

It is important to note that signing English systems are not the same thing as true sign languages, such as American Sign Language (ASL). The striking difference between the two for practitioners is that signing English systems follow the same word order as spoken English. So it is possible to sign and speak at the same time. But the advocates of American Sign Language (ASL) assert that ASL is the natural language of deaf children. Also, it is the most natural and efficient way for deaf students to learn about the world. They argue that signing English systems are not only awkward but also very difficult to use because they put such a heavy strain on a person's memory. It will be interesting to see over the next several years how successful ASL proponents are in replacing signing English systems.

TECHNOLOGICAL ADVANCES

A number of technological advances have made it easier for hearing impaired children to communicate with hearing people. This explosion of technology has taken place primarily in four areas. The four areas are:

1. Computer assisted Instruction.
2. Television,
3. Telephone, and
4. Hearing aid.

COMPUTER-ASSISTED INSTRUCTION

Many professionals advocate microcomputers as an excellent means of teaching hearing impaired children. There are programmes for teaching reading, writing, and sign language. This programme allows the children to type a sequence of words, or a sentence that appears on the screen, along with a picture of the sentence and the appropriate signs. Researchers are working on computers that will display in visual form the speech produced by the individuals. Visual displays of speech can help deaf children learn to speak better. Work is being done on developing interactive videodisc systems to help hearing people learn sign language.

TELEVISION CAPTIONING AND TELETEXT

There are two types television captions-open and closed. Open captions were used with certain programmes in the 1970s. They were seen on all television screens. Their use was short-lived. The main reason was that the general viewing audience complained that they were distracting. Closed captions became available in 1980s. These captions are visible only on television sets equipped with a special decoder.

Some hearing impaired children are also taking advantage of tele-text, which provides access to such information as news, cultural calendars, and community announcements through television.

TELEPHONE ADAPTATIONS

Hearing impaired children have problems in using telephones because of acoustic feedback, noise from the closeness of the telephone receiver to their hearing aids, and the fact that speech-reading cues can not be used. The development of the teletypewriter, which connects with a phone, is a welcome aid for hearing impaired students. The teletypewriter allows the hearing impaired children to communicate through type with anyone who also has teletypewriter.

HEARING AIDS

There are various kinds of hearing aids, which differ in size, cost, and efficiency. These hearing aides range from wearable hearing aids to group auditory training units, which can be used by a number of children at a time. The wearable hearing aid is the most familiar type known to the public. It comes in a number of models. Some can be inserted within the external auditory canal, some are built into glasses and some can be placed behind the ear. The most powerful kind of wearable aid contains a unit worn on the clothing with an attached earpiece. In general, the more inconspicuous the hearing aid is, the less powerful it is. But the recent advances in the manufacture of miniature transistors have boosted up the efficiency of very small units dramatically. This has resulted in a market increase in the use of in-the-ear and behind-the-ear hearing aids, especially the former, which will become even more popular in the years to come.

Group auditory trainers are used in school situations in which amplification is provided for a group of children. Group trainers need not be small enough to wear. So they are usually more powerful and give better sound quality than the most advanced individual hearing aids.

Hearing aids are an integral part of educational programmes for hearing impaired children; some deaf children can not benefit from them due to the severity and /or kind of their impairment. Generally, hearing aids make sounds louder, not clearer. So, if a person's hearing is distorted, hearing aid will not be of much use. The sound amplified by the hearing aid will be heard by him distorted. For those who can benefit from hearing aids, it is very important for the children, parents, and teachers to work together to ensure the maximum effectiveness of the hearing aid. It is also important for the teacher to monitor the children's use of the hearing aids closely to make sure that they are using the hearing aids consistently and that the aids are operating appropriately.

TEACHING HEARING IMPAIRED STUDENTS IN GENERAL EDUCATION CLASSROOMS

Children with mild hearing losses usually attend schools for several years before their hearing impairments are identified. Some of them soon learn to compensate for their hearing difficulties in many school situations. However, they are at a disadvantage when compared academically with their normal nondisabled classmates. Also, they are at risk to become frustrated learners and socially isolated from other students. That is why the teacher must be aware of the following indicators of a possible hearing loss. It is very important for the teacher to look for the following indicators of possible hearing loss so that he can design his intervention programmes appropriately.

1. Hearing impaired children experience considerable difficulties in understanding spoken language and /or in speaking.
2. They remain absent frequently because of ear aches, sinus congestion, allergies, and related conditions.
3. They are often inattentive and day dreaming in the classroom.
4. They evince disorientation and /or confusion, especially when noise levels are high.
5. They find it very difficult to follow directions.
6. They tend to imitate other students' behaviour in the classroom

If these signs occur consistently, the classroom teacher can easily identify the hearing impaired children. Such students can be referred to a speech and language specialist who will administer tests to determine whether or not there is a hearing loss. Once they are confirmed and classified as hearing impaired children, their specific needs should be assessed and educational programmes should be designed accordingly.

Teaching Techniques to Try

Regular curriculum may be introduced to those hearing impaired students who are mainstreamed. At the same time, some students with hearing losses may require modifications of the physical, instructional, and social environments to derive maximum benefits from general education.

Modifications of Physical Environment

The following modifications of physical environment are very essential to enhance the learning of hearing, impaired children in general education classroom.

1. The teacher may make changes in seating, such as moving students away from such sources of background noise as open windows and doors and noisy hearing and cooling systems.

2. The teacher can seat the hearing impaired students in the front of the room with their chairs or desks turned slightly so that they can see the faces of all other students.
3. The teacher can permit free movement around the classroom, so that hearing impaired children can reduce the distance between themselves and the speakers.
4. Hearing impaired students may be allowed to change their seats as activities change.
5. Positioning of speakers is also very important. Their faces must be illuminated even when the room is darkened for studies, videotapes, and films. This will facilitate speechreading.
6. Classroom for hearing impaired students must be located away from high traffic and noise areas such as groups, cafeterias and playgrounds.
7. Though expensive, the school authorities can take effort to reduce classroom noise by carpeting floors, draping windows and covering walls with materials that absorb extraneous noise such as corkboard or Styrofoam sheets.

INSTRUCTIONAL MODIFICATIONS

Instructional modifications are very essential to accentuate the learning of hearing impaired children. The teacher should use teaching formats that include exhibits, demonstrations, experiments and simulations. These provide hands-on experiences that tend to promote understanding and are easier to follow than lectures and whole-class discussions. The teacher can write directions in short, simple sentences and use pictures to illustrate the procedure or process. This will supplement the oral explanations during demonstrations.

When the teacher uses lecture and discussion formats, he can pretutor students by having them read ahead or work with another student to become familiar with the new concepts and information that will be discussed. Kampfe (1984), Palmer (1988) and Ross (1982) recommend the following techniques to promote understanding of hearing impaired children during lectures and discussions.

- The teacher can use an overhead projector to note important points so that he can face students while lecturing.

- The teacher must avoid moving around the room while speaking so that the students can see his or her face.
- The teacher should shorten or simplify verbalisation.
- The teacher should repeat all the main points.
- The teacher should provide nonverbal cues and use facial expressions, body movements, and gestures.
- He should call the speakers' names so that the time spent in locating the source of speech can be reduced.
- The students can be asked to raise their hands so that the noise and confusion that results from several people talking at once can be avoided.

MODIFICATION OF ORAL COMMUNICATION

Garwood (1987) suggests a mnemonic device to improve oral instruction with hearing impaired students.

S= State the topic to be discussed.
P= Pace your conversation at a moderate speed with occasional pauses to permit comprehension.
E = Enunciate clearly, without exaggerated lip movements.
E = Enthusiastically communicate, using body language and natural gestures.
CH = Check comprehension before changing topics.

MODIFICATION OF WRITTEN MATERIALS

Besides modifying oral communication, it is very important to modify written materials by using graphic pictorial forms such as diagrams, pictures, graphs, and graphic outlines. A sound instructional format with deaf students is predominantly pictorial with some verbal information. Adapting materials in this way will reduce the language and reading demands and the amount of content the hearing impaired students may find difficult to cover, especially in high school classes in which the reading requirements are substantiated.

PEER TUTORING

Regardless of the teaching format the teacher uses, he must follow a preview, teach, and review cycle. The teacher can arrange for student tutors to assist in this process so that the hearing impaired students can benefit socially as well as academically from tutoring by a classmate. The student tutors can preview materials by pointing out main points and new vocabulary before the lesson is presented. After the teacher presents the lesson, the student tutor can review the material providing additional examples, practice and classification, as needed. This system will enable the hearing impaired children to develop a better insight into the concept.

BUDDY SYSTEM

Teachers can use the buddy system to create other opportunities for social and academic interactions. In this arrangement a normal student with no hearing problem sits next to a student with hearing loss to clarify explanations directions, page numbers, and other oral communications Buddies can share class notes so that hearing impaired students can concentrate on the speaker. Both peer tutoring and buddy arrangements are very useful to encourage increased communication and social interactions between students.

SUMMARY

Speech and language are tools used for purposes as of communication. Speech is the behaviour of forming and sequencing the sounds of oral language. Speech disorders are impairments in the production and use of oral language. They include disabilities in producing voice, making speech sounds (articulation), and producing speech with a normal flow (fluency).

Speech disorders can be classified on the basis of etiology according to which it may be organic or functional. Organic group includes speech disorders caused by palatal anomalies, dental irregularities, paralysis and tumours of larynx, brain damage etc. Functional group represents failure to learn speech due to general personality and emotional disturbances. But this dichotomy is not crystal clear.

Speech disorders can be classified according to the major symptoms as voice disorders, articulation disorders, delayed speech and fluency disorders. There are various causes of speech impairment. They are organic causes, functional causes, psychogenic causes, psychological causes, loss of hearing, social influences, and cerebral palsy.

Educational programmes for speech impaired children include speech therapy, articulation correction, speech training activities, extra-curricular activities and co-operative learning.

There are many definitions and classification systems of hearing important. By far the most common division is between deaf and hard of hearing. Children who can not hear sounds at or above a certain intensity (loudness) level are classified as deaf; others with a hearing loss are classified as hard of hearing.

Common characteristics of hearing impaired children include linguistic difficulties, problem in personal and social adjustment, personality problems, abnormal emotional behaviour and psychological complex.

Conducted loss, Sensorineural impairments, mixed impairments and impairments of the middle ear, are some causes of hearing impairments. These children can be identified by following techniques such as systematic observation, case study, hearing tests and school screening.

Educational programmes for hearing impaired children include oral approach and total communication approach. Oral approach includes auditory training and speech training. Total communication approach makes use of both oral approach and manual approach.

Modifications of physical environment, instructional modifications, modification of oral communication, modification of written materials, peer tutoring and buddy system are some important techniques to teach speech and hearing impaired children in general education classroom.

REFERENCE

Chintamani Kar (1992). *Exceptional Children: Their Psychology and Instruction.* Sterling Publishers, New Delhi.

Garwood, V.P. (1987) Audiology in Public School Setting. In F.N. Martin (Ed) *Hearing Disorders in Children.* Pro-Ed, Austin, TX.

Hallahan, D.P., and Kauffman, J.M. (1991). *Exceptional Children: An Introduction to Special Education.* Prentice - Hall International Editions, London.

Kampfe, C.M. (1984) Mainstreaming Some practices: Suggestions For Teachers and Administrators. In R.H. Hull and K.L. Dilka (Eds.) *The Hearing Impaired Child in School.* Grune and Stratton, Orlando, FL.

Meadow, K.P. (1984) *Deafness and Child Development.* University of California Press, Berkeley.

Palmer, L. (1988) Speechreading as communication. *The Volta Review.*

Ross, M. (1982) *Hard of Hearing Children in Regular Schools.* Prentice-Hall, Englewood Cliffs, NJ.

Sacks, O. (1989) *Seeing Voices: A Journey into the World of Deaf.* University of California Press, Berkeley.

4

MENTALLY RETARDED CHILDREN

OBJECTIVES

This chapter deals with mentally retarded children. The causes and degrees of mental retardation are described. Also, the educational provisions for mentally retarded children are outlined. After reading this chapter, the readers should be able to:

1. Define mental retardation
2. Understnd the causes and degrees of mental retardation.
3. Identify mentally retarded children.
4. Develop an insight into the educational considerations of mentally retarded children.
5. Teach students with mental retardation in general education classroom.

Children with mental retardation may be heartbreakingly different from the children next door in some ways, but also like them in others. Recent research findings indicate that retardation is quantitative rather than qualitative. In many areas mentally retarded children function like a non-disabled child but a non-disabled child at a younger chronological age. Even the differences that do exist need not cause parents a lifetime constant headache. Today many professionals recognise that mental retardation is a socially constructed condition to some extent. It is the individual's social system that determines whether the individual is retarded. Most mentally retarded children, particularly those, who are higher functioning, do not "officially" become retarded until they enter the school. It is because the school as a social system has a certain set of expectations some children do not meet.

DEFINITION OF MENTAL RETARDATION

Mental retardation refers to significantly sub-average intellectual functioning resulting in or associated with impairments in adaptive behaviour and manifested during the developmental period. This definition indicates that a person must be well below average in both measured intelligence and adaptive behaviour to be classified as retarded. At one time mental retardation was diagnosed on the basis of an IQ below 85. But, today they must have deficits in adaptive behaviour and an IQ below 75 or 70. Mental retardation need not be a life-long condition, especially for those whose degree of retardation is relatively mild. Furthermore, early educational programming can prevent some children from being diagnosed so.

ADAPTIVE BEHAVIOUR

Adaptive behaviour plays a vital role in determining whether a person is retarded. Some children may score low on a standardised intelligence test, but have adequate adaptive skills. Some children may function in the retarded range while they are in school for six hours of the day but they may behave normally-adjust and adapt competently-once they return to the home community for the other eighteen hours. Adaptive behaviour encompasses more than the ability to survive outside school. They are different for the preschooler and adult. In infancy and early childhood, sensory-motor, communication, self-help, and socialisation skills are important. In middle childhood and early adolescence, learning abilities and interpersonal social skills are important. In late adolescence and adulthood, vocational skills and social responsibilities are important.

INTELLECTUAL FUNCTIONING

The words "sub-average general intellectual functioning" in the definition refer to scores more than two standard deviations below the mean on a standardised test of intelligence. One commonly used IQ is the Wechsler Intelligence Scale for Children - Revised (WISC-R). On this text, a score of 70 would be two standard deviations below the mean, or average, of 100. The score of seventy may be treated as a guideline but a cutoff of 75 may be warranted in some cases.

CLASSIFICATION OF MENTAL RETARDATION

Most professionals classify mentally retarded individuals according to the severity of their problems. The most generally accepted approach is to classify on the basis of a continuum or scale of severity. The two most common systems of classification are that of the American Association on Mental Retardation (AAMR) and the one used by educators.

THE AAMR CLASSIFICATION

The AAMR classifies mental retardation as mild, moderate, severe, and profound retardation. This classification is made on the basis of IQ range.

MILD MENTAL RETARDATION (I.Q. 50-55 TO 70)

Those individuals who possess IQs between 50-55 and 70 are diagnosed as having mild mental retardation. About 90 percent of mentally retarded people belong to this category. The persons in this group are educable. They evince an organic pathology and require little supervision. With parental assistance and special training, they can be taught to be self-supporting.

MODERATE MENTAL RETARDATION (IQ. 35-40 TO 50-55)

Those individuals who possess IQs between 35-40 and 50-55 are diagnosed as having moderate mental retardation. About 6 percent of the mentally retarded people belong to this category. These individuals are trainable retardates. Their rate of learning is very slow. Physically they appear clumsy and lack motor coordination. Though some of them may require institutionalisation, they can manage to live safely under the protection of their family members.

SEVERE MENTAL RETARDATION (IQ 20-25 TO 35-40)

Those individuals who possess IQs between 20-25 and 35-40 are diagnosed as having severe mental retardation. About 3 percent of the mentally retarded people belong to this category. These individuals are considered dependent retarded. These persons suffer from severe retardation in motor and speech development. Majority of them are permanently institutionalised and require constant care and attention. They can perform simple occupational tasks under supervision.

PROFOUND MENTAL RETARDATION (IQ BELOW 20-25)

Those individuals who possess IQs below 20-25 are diagnosed as having profound mental retardation. About 1 percent of the mentally retarded people belong to this category. They are considered "life support" mental retardates. These persons are severely deficient in adaptive behaviour and unable to do simple tasks. Retarded growth, pathology of central nervous system, mutism, deafness and convulsive seizures are common symptoms of these people. They are unable to look after themselves. They can not attend to their basic physical needs. They need life long support

Most professionals hold that the AAMR classification is the most useful for the following three reasons.

1. The terms used-mid, moderate, severe and profound retardation do not carry the degree of negative stereotyping of earlier descriptions such as "idiot" and "feebleminded".

These adjectives apply to a vast array of other things or conditions besides retardation.

2. The terms used emphasise the level of functioning of the individual.
3. The use of bands of IQ scores for example 50-55 as the cutoff between mild and moderate retardation leaves some room for clinical judgement and recognises that IQ scores are not perfect predictors of a person's level of retardation.

EDUCATORS' CLASSIFICATION

Educators classify mental retarded children as educable mentally retarded (EMR), trainable mentally retarded (TMR), and severely and profoundly handicapped (SPH).

Educable mentally Retarded (EMR) individuals are those who possess IQs between 75-70 and 50. More and more school systems are now using 70, whereas previously they used 75.

Trainable Mentally Retarded (TMR) individuals are those who possess IQs between 50 and 25.

Severely and profoundly handicapped (SPH) individuals are those who possess IQs below 25

The terms "educable" and "trainable" have survived over the years among educators because they describe, albeit grossly, the educational needs of retarded children. In general, children classified as EMR can learn some basic academic subjects. The curriculum for the children classified as TMR, on the other hand, concentrates more on functional academic subjects, with emphasis on self-help and vocational skills.

CAUSES OF MENTAL RETARDATION

Many authorities are of the opinion that it is possible to pinpoint the cause of mental retardation in only about 6 to 15 percent of the cases. Although, there is some overlap, the causal factors for mild retardation differ from those for more severe levels of retardation.

CAUSES OF MILD RETARDATION

Most individuals identified as retarded are classified as mildly retarded. They do not differ from their non-handicapped peers in appearance. They are usually not diagnosed as retarded until they enter school where they begin to fall behind in schoolwork. In addition, in the vast majority of the cases it is not possible to specify the exact cause of retardation. Many professionals believe that the following factors cause mild retardation.

1. Mildly retarded individuals often have cultural familial retardation, which is regarded as a vital causative factor.
2. Genetic factors also cause mild retardation, though they play a vital role in severe retardation.
3. Environmental factors cause mild retardation. Environmental factors presumably cause retardation because they produce such effects as inadequate learning opportunities and poor nutrition. Which causes more retardation heredity or environment has been the subject of debate for years.

CAUSES OF SEVERE RETARDATION

Causes of retardation in individuals classified as moderately retarded and profoundly retarded can more easily be determined than the causes of retardation in individuals classified as mildly retarded. Causes for more severe retardation can be divided into two general categories such as genetic factors and brain damage.

i) Genetic Factors

There are a number of genetically related causes of mental retardation. These are, generally, of two types those that result from some damage to genetic material, such as chromosomal abnormalities, and those that are due to hereditary transmission. Genetic factors include three conditions such as Down Syndrome, which results from chromosomal abnormality, and PKU (Phenylk-etonuria) and Tay-Sachs disease, both of which are inherited.

Down Syndrome accounts for approximately 10 percent of all moderate and severe cases of retardation. Down syndrome is sometimes, though less acceptably, referred to as mongolism because of the facial characteristic of thick epicanthal folds in the corners of the eyes, making them appear to slant upward slightly. Other common physical characteristics include small stature; decreased muscle tone (hypotonia); hyper flexibility of joints; speckling of the iris of the eye; small oral cavity, which results in protruding of the tongue; short and broad hands with a single palmar crease; and a wide gap between the first and second toes. Researchers are coming closer and closer to discovering the exact gene or genes that cause Down Syndrome.

PKU (Phenylketonuria) involves the inability of the body to convert a common dietary substance phenylalanine to tyrosine. Accumulation of phenylalanine results in abnormal brain development. Babies can undergo a screening test for PKU in the first few days after birth. Unless a baby with PKU starts a special diet controlling the intake of phenylalanine in infancy and continues it into middle childhood, the child will usually develop severe retardation. If the diet is stopped at middle childhood, a decrease in IQ may occur. So many authorities stress that the diet should be maintained indefinitely, PKU occurs when the parents are carriers of PKU genes.

Tay-Sachs disease, like PKU, can appear when both mother and father are carriers. It results in progressive brain damage and eventual death. It occurs almost exclusively among Ashkenazi Jews that is, those of European extraction. Public health personnel have used genetic screening programmes to identify carriers. Also, this disease can be detected in utero.

ii) Brain Damage

Brain damage causes severe mental retardation. It can result from a host of factors that fall into two general categories-infections and environmental hazards.

INFECTIONS

Infections that may lead to mental retardation can occur in the mother to be or the infant or young child after birth. Rubella,

(German Measles), syphilis, and herpes simplex in the mother can all cause retardation in the child. Rubella is dangerous during the first three months pregnancy. The venereal diseases, syphilis and herpes simplex present a greater risk at later stages of fetal development. These diseases cause brain damage, which, in turn, result in mental retardation.

There are three examples of infections of the children that can affect mental development. They are meningitis encephalitis, and pediatric AIDS

Meningitis is an infection of the covering of the brain that may be caused by a variety of bacterial or viral agents.

Encephalitis is an inflammation of the brain, which results more often in retardation and usually affects intelligence more severely.

Pediatric AIDS is the fastest growing infectious cause of mental retardation. In fact, researchers indicate that it may soon become the leading cause of mental retardation and brain damage. Research studies project that the vast majority of children with pediatric AIDS have got their infection during birth from their mothers, who used intravenous drugs or were sexually active with infected men.

ENVIRONMENTAL HAZARDS

Environmental hazards that can result in mental retardation are a blow to the head, poisons, radiation, malnutrition, prematurity or postmaturity, and birth injury. These can result in mild retardation in some cases. But in most cases these environmental hazards cause severe mental retardation.

A blow to a child's head can result in mental retardation. Child abuse is a cause of brain damage that results in mental retardation and other disabilities.

Poisoning resulting in mental retardation can occur in the expectant mother or in the child. The recent studies have brought to light the harmful effects of a variety of substances, from obvious toxic agents such as cocaine and heroin to more subtle potential "poisons" such as tobacco, alcohol, caffeine, and even food additives. Especially, the pregnant women who smoke and/ or consume alcohol have a greater risk of having babies with behavioural and physical problems.

Radiation is another hazard to the unborn fetus. Pregnant women should not be exposed to x-rays unless absolutely necessary. There are potential dangers of radiation from improperly designed or supervised nuclear power plants.

Improper nutrition also causes mental retardation. When the expectant mother is malnourished or when the child once born does not have a proper diet, retardation occurs.

Abnormal length of pregnancy either too short (prematurity) or too long (post maturity) can also result in mental retardation. The latter is not likely to cause retardation but it is possible that the fetus will suffer from poor nutrition, if it is long overdue. Both premature and small (underweight infant) suffer from physical or behavioural abnormalities including retardation. Poor nutrition, teenage pregnancy, drug abuse, and excessive cigarette smoking are some causative factors of prematurity.

CHARACTERISTICS OF MENTALLY RETARDED CHILDREN

There are various psychological and behavioural characteristics associated with mentally retarded children. But it can not be said with certain that each mentally retarded child will display all the characteristics mentioned. There is a great deal of variability in the behaviour of retarded children. Each retarded person is a unique and separate individual. The characteristics of mentally retarded children are classified into two types as cognitive characteristics and personality characteristics.

i) Cognitive Characteristics

The most obvious characteristics of mentally retarded children are their reduced ability to learn. There are quite a number of ways in which mentally retarded children exhibit cognitive problems. Research has documented four areas in which the mentally retarded children are likely to have difficulties. The four areas are attention, memory, language, and academics.

ATTENTION DEFICIT

The importance of attention for learning is critical. Children must be able to attend to the task at hand before they can learn it. Many of the problems of mentally retarded children can be attributed to attention problems. They often attend to the wrong things and they experience difficulty in allocating their attention properly. Mentally retarded children have less attention to allocate to different processes and they can not efficiently assign the proper amount or quality of attention to the various aspects of a task.

POOR MEMORY

Researchers have posited that mentally retarded children do more poorly than the non-disabled children when asked to remember a list of words or sounds or group of pictures presented a few seconds earlier. This can be ascribed to their poor processing of information. Depth of processing is very essential to remember certain material. Research has demonstrated that the deeper the level of processing is required, the greater the memory problems the mentally retarded children will have. In other words, the more complicated the memory task is, the more likely the retarded children will have difficulties with it.

One of the primary reasons for mentally retarded children to have problems on more complicated memory tasks is that they have difficulty in using efficient learning strategies. Many authorities have attributed mentally retarded children's inefficient use of learning strategies such as rehearsal and clustering to the fact that their executive control processes are less well developed. But even though retarded children are deficient in the spontaneous use of learning strategies and executive control processes, they can be taught to use such processes successfully.

INADEQUATE LANGUAGE DEVELOPMENT

Many mentally retarded children have language and speech problems, for example, articulation errors. The greater the degree of retardation is, the more severe the difficulties are. In general, the language of mentally retarded children, especially those classified as mildly retarded, follows the same developmental course as that of non-retarded children. However, the language development progresses at a slower rate. The severely retarded children exhibit inadequate language development.

POOR ACADEMIC PERFORMANCE

As there is a strong relationship between intelligence and achievement, it is not surprising that many retarded students lag behind their non-retarded peers in all areas of achievement. They also tend to be underachievers in relation to expectations based on their intellectual level. Their learning depends more on rote memory than on understanding. They are found to repeat the errors again and again. They face difficulties in engaging in abstract and critical thinking, employing critical judgement, avoiding errors, and in exercising foresight. All these factors contribute to their poor academic performance.

PERSONALITY CHARACTERISTICS

Mentally retarded children display certain unique personality characteristics. Some of them are briefly discussed below.

SOCIAL AND EMOTIONAL INADEQUACY

Mentally retarded children evince social and emotional problems especially; they experience problems in making friends, and have poor self-concepts. There are two reasons why they are so. First, some of their behaviour may "turn off" their peers. For example, mentally retarded children engage in higher rates of inattention and disruptive behaviour than their non-retarded classmates. Second, their non-retarded classmates may despise them, as they do not want to have any association with individuals who are retarded. As a result, the mentally retarded children encounter problems in social interaction with others.

LACK OF MOTIVATION

In addition to social emotional problems, mentally retarded children exhibit motivation problems. These children tend to lack confidence in their own abilities. They believe that they have little control over what happens to them. They also think that they are primarily controlled by other people or events. As such, they have a tendency to give up easily when faced with challenging tasks.

LIMITED INDIVIDUAL DIFFERENCES

It is a known fact that no two individuals in this world have the same personality. But in case of mentally retarded children, there appear to be less prominent individual differences. These children do not exhibit such marked individual differences as non-retarded children do. Among the retardates, it is rare to find individuals who may be described as dynamic, charming, forceful, vicious, obnoxious or outstanding. Many mentally retarded children are colourless and tractable.

ORGANISMIC INFERIORITY

Mentally retarded children suffer from general structural and functional inferiority of the entire organism. These children learn to talk and walk at a much later stage. Defective speech and shuffling gait are two very prominent characteristics of these children. When compared with their non-retarded peers, their sensory discrimination is less acute. The retardates are relatively insensitive to pain and their auditory and visual defects are common. It is very rare to find normal performance among mental retardates, who fall short of normal performance on tests of mechanical ability.

ADJUSTMENT PROBLEM

Mentally retarded children experience mild depression, feelings of worthlessness and helplessness. As these children grow older, they become lonely and unable to adjust in society. Research evidence indicates that frustration of psychological and social needs predisposes some retarded children to feel angry and rebellious Very often, the parents of mentally retarded children develop a guilt complex. Parental overprotection is a good example for this. Often they do not encourage self-help; rather they continue to dress and feed the child up to an advanced age. Consequently, this type of behaviour fosters a dependent style of interaction in the retardates. Thus overprotection and denial of the parents result in adjustment difficulties of such type of children.

IDENTIFYING MENTALLY RETARDED CHILDREN

Professionals measure two major areas to determine whether the children are mentally retarded: intelligence and adaptive behaviour. So the teachers can easily identify mentally retarded children by administering intelligence tests and by assessing adaptive behaviour.

INTELLIGENCE TESTS

There are various types of IQ tests. Because of their accuracy and predictive capabilities, practitioners prefer individually administered tests to group tests. Individual tests are very useful to diagnose a child for placement in a special education programme. Stanford-Binet and the Wechsler Intelligence Scale for Children - Revised (WISC-R) are the two most common individual IQ tests for children. Both Stanford Binet and WISC-R are verbal. WISC-R has a verbal and a performance scale with a number of sub-tests. The verbal and performance IQ measures are sometimes compared to scores on the subtests for purposes of educational programming. Any of these two tests can be administered and the children can be identified on the basis of their IQ.

ASSESSING ADAPTIVE BEHAVIOUR

There are numerous adaptive behaviour measures available. Two of the most commonly used measures are AAMD Adaptive Behaviour Scale - School Edition (Lambert and Windmiller, 1981) and the Adaptive Behaviour Inventory. For Children

(ABIC) (Mercer and Lewis, 1977). The AAMD scale has two sections, one for daily living skills and one for personality and behaviour. The ABIC assesses adaptive behaviour in six areas: family, community, peer relations, non-academic school roles, easier-consumer, and self-maintenance.

EDUCATION OF MENTAL RETARDATES

Although there is some overlap, in general the focus of educational programmes varies according to whether the children are mildly, moderately, or severely and profoundly retarded. For example, the lesser the degree of retardation, the more the teacher emphasises academic skills, and the greater the degree of retardation the more stress there is on self-help, community living, and vocational skills. It should be remembered that this distinction is largely a matter of emphasis. In actual classroom practice, all teachers of retarded students need to teach academic, self-help, community living, and vocational skills irrespective of the severity levels of their students. A brief description of the major features of educational programmes for educable mentally retarded, trainable mentally retarded and severely and profoundly retarded children is presented below.

EDUCATION OF EDUCABLE MENTALLY RETARDED

Researchers are of the opinion that educable mentally retarded children tend to fail in an ordinary school. Nevertheless, they are capable of making progress in normal schools. The schools should provide them with such curriculum and methodology of teaching that will enable them to surmount their difficulties easily. It should be the first priority of the teacher to help the mentally, retarded children to become self-sufficient and an accepted adult member of the community in which he lives. The special methods adapted in teaching the educable mentally retarded are as follows:

I) Individualisation

Individualisation of education is obviously the dominant theme that comes to mind when we think of special methods of instructing the educable mentally retarded children.

Individualisation of education does not mean that children receive individual instructions with small classes, but it implies that each child is allowed to proceed at his own pace of learning according to his own unique growth pattern. At the same time, these children must be provided with opportunities for group participation so that correct social attitudes can be developed in them.

ii) Learning by Doing

The implication of the principle of learning by doing can not be underestimated in teaching the educable mentally retarded children. The basic principle of special education has always been that the children should learn by doing. Teachers should give top priority to activity methods that lay emphasis on learning through experience. Generally the deficiency of mentally retarded children lies in the area of relational and abstract thought. So these children encounter problems in learning where the mode of communication is largely verbal. It has been posited that these children learn better through such materials that appeal most to their senses.

iii) Need for Learning Readiness

While introducing academic work to mentally retarded children, teachers should give due importance to the concept of maturation and readiness to learn. These children have the potential to learn to read, but they should be prepared through appropriate readiness programmes. It is always rewarding to wait until the children are intellectually and psychologically ready to accept the challenging task.

iv) Graded Curriculum

These is no denying that these retarded children learn more slowly than average children. It warrants careful gradation of subjects. It poses problems for the teachers who have to shoulder the responsibilities of grading the curriculum and preparing the study materials for them. It is, no doubt, a tough task for the already overburdened teachers, but not an impossible task.

v) Repetition

Mentally retarded children are known for poor memory. For them, teaching method must provide for a considerable amount of repetition so that they can retain the learned material in their memory. The children should have clear understanding of the materials before facing any retention test. The memory span of these retarded children can be enhanced by imbibing in them interest and motivation. Research studies have posited that the memory spans of retarded children, increases, if the learning materials have meaningful associations.

vi) Periods of Short Duration

Mentally retarded children can not concentrate on a subject for a longer time. They have limited power of concentration. They can not concentrate on them for more than 20 minutes or so. For this reason, formal teaching periods should be fairly short. It is of prime importance to consider how long children can concentrate when the subject is stimulating. Modular instruction with appropriate teacher support system will be very effective for retarded children.

vii) Concrete Problems

There is no doubt that mentally retarded children lack imagination and foresight. As a result, they experience considerable difficulty in transferring the learning experience of one situation to another situation that is similar but new. To overcome this problem, they need concrete presentation of instruction. Real life problems should be introduced whenever possible so that the teachers can ensure immediate application of learning experiences.

viii) Projects

"Introduction of projects" or "centres of interest" is a significant approach for teaching mentally retarded children. Researchers are trying to establish how this can be done without serious disruption of the basic subject programme. It is not the teachers who should introduce the topics around which centres interest grow and develop but it is the topic that should arise spontaneously out of the classroom situation where the manifestation of further information is clear. The point of origin may be a short story, a poem, a song, a film or picture in a magazine or newspaper. It is not necessary to give underimportance to the source, but it requires expertise on the part of the teacher to present it through careful planning and guidance.

EDUCATION OF TRAINABLE MENTALLY RETARDED

The trainable mentally retarded children have I.Q in the range of 25-50. These children are much more retarded than educable mentally retarded children. So it is important to frame a different educational structure and curriculum for these children. The main objective of education for these children is to enable them to take care of themselves and to do simple occupational jobs. These children have prominent physical anomalies such as seizures, lack of control over elimination etc. It makes regular schooling difficult for these children. So primary objective should be to train these retarded children how to do their daily work without the help of others. These daily works include working, dressing themselves, eating properly, doing simple jobs and toilet training etc.

In the education of trainable mentally retarded children less importance is given to teaching of academic subjects and more time is devoted to the development of sensorimotor, self-care, and daily living skills. As these children become tired very soon, a more definite timetable is necessary with short periods of activity. Therefore the curriculum for the trainable mentally retarded children should include the following.

i) Self-care

The curriculum should focus on a programme of simple habit training. This will enable those children to develop skills of self-help with regard to their daily practical needs. Teachers should adapt such methods for this purpose that relate to the real life experiences and everyday needs of the children.

ii) Social training

Teachers of these children should give priority to group activities such as games, simple dramatic work, and story telling etc. This will enable them to interact with others, which is essential for socialisation. This will also increase gregariousness and affiliation. The children become generally active and cooperative. This provides training in adjustment also.

iii) Sensory Training

Teachers should lay much emphasis on such instructions that will enable the retarded children to make the fullest use of their senses. This is very required to make them self-reliant and more sociable. Proper sensory training will contribute to the development of social skills in these retarded children.

iv) Language Development

Teachers should provide them with such aids that will ensure better speech development in them. The degree of their socialisation depends on the degree of their language development. They should be able to follow directions and interact with peers in group situation. These children should be taught reading in order to enable them to function independently.

v) Craft work and Music

For developing a sense of self-confidence in trainable mentally retarded, the curriculum should include simple crafts training programmes like weaving, rug making, basketing etc. This will enable these children to attain economic self-sufficiency in adulthood. Research evidence has brought to light that music is sometimes found as a means of releasing their energy and provides a form of expression, which the mentally retarded children enjoy. So music should be given appropriate importance in the curriculum.

EDUCATION FOR SEVERELY AND PROFOUNDLY RETARDED CHILDREN

Most authorities agree that the following features should characterise the educational programmes for severely and profoundly retarded children.

i) Age-appropriate curriculum and materials
ii) Functional activities
iii) Community based instruction
iv) Integrated therapy
v) Interaction with non-retarded peers
vi) Family involvement

AGE-APPROPRIATE CURRICULUM AND MATERIALS

In the past there was a tendency to "baby" even older severely and profoundly retarded persons because of their intellectual limitations. Authorities are of the opinion now that this is not only demeaning but also educationally harmful. Using infantile materials works against the goal of fostering as much independent behaviour as possible. So the curriculum and the instructional material must be appropriate to the age of the students.

FUNCTIONAL ACTIVITIES

Educational programmes for severely and profoundly retarded children focuses on preparing them to live as independently as possible so much, that activities should be practical. Learning to dress oneself by practising on a doll, for example, is not as effective as practising with one's own dress. Some severely and profoundly retarded children may be able to learn some academic skills. Teaching these children basic reading and math is very time consuming. It is, therefore, very important to teach them only what they will need and what they can learn.

COMMUNITY BASED INSTRUCTION

In keeping with the notion of functional skills, educational programmes for severely and profoundly retarded children need to take place in the community as much as possible. Because many of the skills they learn are for use in settings outside the classroom, such as public transportation, or the grocery store, instruction in such activities has proved more effective when done in those settings. The teacher may wish to use simulated experiences in the classroom, by creating a "mini-grocery" store with a couple of aisles of products and a cash register, for example, to prepare students before they go to a real store. But such simulations themselves will not be of much use for severely and profoundly retarded children who very much need the actual experience of going into those settings in which they will need to use the skills they are learning.

INTEGRATED THERAPY

Many severely and profoundly retarded children have multiple disabilities that necessitate the services of a variety of professionals, such as speech, physical and occupational therapists. Many authorities are of the opinion that these professionals should rather integrate what they do with students into the overall educational programme than doing their job alone in a therapy room. For example, they point out that it would be better to teach retarded children how to walk up and down the actual stairs in the school they actually attend instead of using the specially made stairs placed in therapy rooms for this purpose.

INTERACTION WITH NON-DISABLED STUDENTS

Most authorities concur that it is beneficial for both severely and profoundly retarded children and their non-retarded peers to interact. One method used by some schools is to engage non-disabled students to act as tutors or classroom helpers in classes for severely and profoundly retarded students. This interaction facilitates normalisation or socialisation of retarded students.

FAMILY INVOLVEMENT

Research findings point out that family involvement is very essential for the success of educational programmes for disabled students of all types and severity levels. It is particularly very important for severely and profoundly retarded students. It is because many of the skills they are taught in the classroom will be used in their homes. The involvement can range from merely informing parents about the progress of their children to having them out as classroom aides.

USING APPLIED BEHAVIOUR ANALYSIS TO TEACH RETARDED CHILDREN

Applied behaviour Analysis is effectively used with all types of disabled students, but it is particularly of much value to teach retarded students, especially those with more severe learning problems. Applied behaviour analysis is the application and evaluation of principles of learning theory in teaching situations. It consists of six steps (see Table 4.1)

First, the teacher identifies the overall goal. This is usually a skill area the student needs more work in or an inappropriate behaviour that he needs to decrease. Second, further information is obtained on the identified skill area or behaviour by taking a baseline measurement. The baseline measurement indicates at what level the student is currently functioning. The teacher can later compare the student's performance after instruction with the original baseline performance. Third, the teacher decides on a specific learning objective; that is, the teacher breaks down the overall goal into specific skills the child is to learn. Fourth, the teacher implements an intervention designed to increase needed skills or decrease inappropriate behaviour, for example, a drill and practice routine for math problems or a reward system for good behaviour. Fifth, the child's progress is monitored by measuring performance frequently, usually daily. Sixth, the teacher evaluates the effects of the intervention, usually by charting the student's performance during intervention and comparing it with the baseline performance. Based on this evaluation, the teacher decides whether to continue, modify, or end the intervention.

TEACHING RETARDED CHILDREN IN GENERAL EDUCATION CLASSROOM

What to Look for in School

Children with moderate and severe and profound mental retardation can be identified even before they enter the school, but the children who are mildly retarded can be identified during the school years. Like learning disabled students, mildly retarded children also experience considerable difficulties in attention, language and memory. For example, these retarded students find it very difficult to begin assignments properly and to stay on task. Also, they develop motor, language, social and independent skills more slowly than most students in their class. Moreover, those mildly mentally retarded children have short-term memory problems and they do not know how to use learning strategies that their non-disabled peers seem to use spontaneously.

Furthermore, these mildly retarded students usually experience difficulty in learning in all academic areas, and their rate of skill acquisition is much slower than their non-disabled peers. However, teachers can adopt certain teaching techniques so as to help these retarded children master many of the concepts and skills presented in elementary school.

To achieve this goal, the teachers should

- Divide learning materials into small segments or steps.
- Carefully sequence these steps from simplest to most difficult.
- Use concrete examples and experiences to teach concepts.
- Teach learning strategies
  Provide much drill and practice to promote mastery.
  Give consistent feedback and reinforcement.

TEACHING TECHNIQUES TO TRY

In addition to applied behaviour analysis discussed earlier in this chapter, teachers can try peer tutoring technique, reverse mainstreaming technique and modular instruction, with active teacher support system.

PEER TUTORING

Mentally retarded children in a large heterogeneous class need repeated practice and individual help. To provide practice and adequate help, teachers can make use of tutoring, a technique that under certain conditions have been shown to benefit both tutor and tutee academically, behaviourally, and socially. In peer tutoring programmes teachers typically provide instruction to all class members. Then the students in the class (peer tutors) or older students (cross age tutors) who have mastered the learning are engaged to assist those students in need of additional instruction and practice during regularly scheduled tutorial sessions. Tutors have to perform many tasks such as reviewing lessons, directing and monitoring the performance of newly learned skills, and providing feedback and reinforcement. It is the duty of the teachers to plan, supervise and evaluate a peer tutoring programme. The following conditions are necessary if peer tutoring is to be effective.

1. Tutor training includes such skills as understanding the instructional objective(s), discrimination between correct and incorrect responses, delivery of corrective feedback and reinforcement, monitoring progress and record keeping, and appropriate interpersonal skills.
2. Well-defined behavioural objectives reflect the regular class curriculum.
3. Instructional steps are carefully sequenced and clearly outlined in a lesson format so those tutors can follow easily.
4. Instruction continues in a single skill or concept until the tutor has mastered that learning,
5. Easily identifiable tutee responses are required that tutors can consistently recognise and then correct or reinforce.
6. Tutors monitor and record tutee performance on instructional objectives during each session.
7. Teachers actively monitor both tutor and tutee performance frequently.
8. Teacher deliver frequent reinforcement consistently to the tutor and the tutee contingent on their appropriate performance.
9. Tutorial sessions are scheduled at least two or three times each week; each meeting lasting approximately fifteen to thirty minutes.
10. Tutors provide examples from all settings in which tutees are to use the learning.

REVERSE MAINSTREAMING

Another educational arrangement in which students help other students is reverse mainstreaming. This programme involves a few non-disabled students participating in some of the activities conducted in special education classrooms. Their participation helps disabled students learn appropriate behaviours such as social and language skills while promoting within the non-handicapped children an awareness of special education students and classes. Teachers select non-disabled student volunteers who demonstrate socially appropriate behaviours. After providing them with adequate training and information about special needs children, teacher engages them on tutoring task. In one reverse mainstreaming programme, Project Special Friend, volunteers interacted with severely retarded children. The programme was quite successful in imbibing in retarded children appropriate behaviours.

SUMMARY

Children with mental retardation may be markedly different from the children next door in some ways, but also like them in others. Mental retardation is a socially constructed condition to some extent. Most mentally retarded children are easily identified when they enter the school because the school as a social system has a certain set of expectations some children do not meet.

Mental retardation refers to significantly sub average intellectual functioning resulting in or associated with impairments in adaptive behaviour and manifested during the developmental period.

The AAMR Classifies mental retardation as mild, moderate, severe, and profound retardation. This classification is made on the basis of IQ range. Educators classify mentally retarded children as educable mentally retarded (EMR), trainable mentally retarded (TMR) and severely and profoundly handicapped.

Causes of mental retardation include cultural familial retardation, genetic factors, environmental factors, and brain damage. Attention deficits, poor memory, inadequate language development, poor academic performance, social and emotional inadequacy, lack of motivation, organizing inferiority, adjustment problem are some important characteristics of mentally retarded children.

Educational considerations of educable mentally retarded include individualisation, learning by doing, ensuring learning readiness, graded curriculum, repetition, periods of short duration, concrete problems and projects. Educational programmes for trainable mentally retarded children include self-care, social training, sensory training, language development craftwork and music.

Age-appropriate curriculum and materials, functional activities, community based instruction, integrated therapy, interaction with non-retarded peers, and family involvement should characterise the educational programmes for severely and profoundly retarded children. Peer tutoring and reverse mainstreaming are useful techniques to teach mentally retarded children in general education classrooms.

REFERENCE

Blake K.A. (1976). *The Mentally Retarded: An Educational Psychology.* Prentice Hall, New Delhi.

Chintamani Kar (1992). *"Exceptional Children: Their Psychology and Instruction"*. Sterling Publishers, New Delhi.

Hallahan, D.P, and kauffman, J.M. (1991) *Exceptional Children: Introduction to Special Education.* Prentice-hall, London.

5

SLOW LEARNERS

OBJECTIVES

This chapter deals with the concept, causes and characteristics of slow learners. Also, the educational programmes to circumvent slow learning are also delineated. After reading this chapter, the readers should be able to:

1. Understand the concept and causes of slow learning.
2. Define slow learners
3. Enumerate the characteristics of slow learners
4. Identify slow learners using both informal and formal measures.
5. Design special educational programmes to circumvent slow learning.

The experience of educators confirms that there are many children who are so backward in basic subjects that they need special help. These pupils have limited scope for achievement. They have intelligence quotients between 76 and 89 and they constitute about 18 percent of the total school population. These students do not stand out as very different from their classmates except that they are always slow on the uptake and are often teased by the other students because of their slowness. They are quite well built physically but rather clumsy and uncoordinated in movement. They are no trouble in school. Although much of the work is too difficult for them, they are patient and co-operative. Some of them are much more limited in their capabilities and some have additional handicaps in physical, environmental, emotional aspects which impede their school progress and personal development. They need special help in the form of special class in ordinary school. Most of the slow learners struggle along in ordinary classes failing to have the special attention which they need.

Their ability to deal with abstract and symbolic materials, (I.e. language, number and concepts) is very limited and their reasoning in practical situation is inferior to that of average students. These pupils differ slightly from normal students in learning ability. They are also unable to deal with relatively complex games and school assignments. They need much external stimulation and encouragement to do simple type of work. These students who are known to be slow to 'catch on' are called slow learners.

DEFINITION OF SLOW LEARNERS

Burt (1937) has rightly pointed out that the term 'backward' or 'slow learner' is reserved for those children who are unable to cope with the work normally expected of their age group. In teaching backward children, the mental age is often taken as a guide to the levels of attainment to be expected of pupils. Thus, if a child's mental age is 10 years, we assume that his attainment age should also be at the 10 year level. On the contrary, if his attainment age falls below his mental age he is considered a slow learner. Jenson (1980) states that students with IQ 80 to 90 who are traditionally labelled 'dull normal' are generally slower to 'catch on' to whatever is being taught if it involves symbolic, abstract or conceptual subject matter. In the early grades in school, they most often have problems in reading and arithmetic and are labelled 'slow learners'. But it is really not that they learn so slowly as that they lag behind in developmental readiness to grasp the concepts that are within easy reach of the majority of their age mates. So they may be called rather 'slow developers' than slow learners.

According to Kirk (1962) the slow learners, average and gifted students can be classified according to their rate of learning. He also strictly refused to equate slow learners with mentally retarded because the former is capable of achieving a reasonable degree of academic success even though at a slower rate than the average student. As an adult, a slow learner usually becomes self supporting, independent and socially adjusted, but in the early stage, he adapts himself to regular classroom programmes which fit in with his slower learning ability. These slow learners are markedly different from under achievers and learning disabled.

CHARACTERISTICS OF SLOW LEARNERS

Taking the aforesaid factors into consideration, characteristics of slow learners can be systematically listed out.

a) Limited Cognitive Capacity

Schonell (1942) defines general intelligence as an inborn, all round mental power which is but slightly altered in degree by environmental influences although its realisation and direction are determined by experience. Intelligence is viewed not merely as an unfolding or maturing of this innate potentiality but also as something that grows and develops in the course of the child's active experience of his environment. This is what the slow learners lack. Due to limited cognitive capacity, slow learners fail to cope with learning situations and to reason abstractly. Rational thinking becomes practically impossible for them.

Slow Learners experience difficulty with the complex mental operation of reasoning. They are usually slower to observe the features of things and to perceive relationships between things in their experience. So they are very poor in the process of developing concepts or general ideas which underlie a great deal of school work, especially in language and number. At the most, they can succeed in rote learning. They evince interest in learning where relationships are clearly demonstrated. With regard to retentive memories they require more practice and revision when compared with normal students. Also, they are poor in employing cognitive strategies which are very essential to facilitate retention processes. These strategies reflect planned and goal directed behaviour and involve cognitive control processes known as executive function, that focus on the retrieval of information from long term memory. Slow Learners do not have adequate cognitive development since they possess limited cognitive capacity. Due to this limited cognitive capacity they are unable to keep pace with their age group.

b) Poor Memory

Burt (1946) remarks that of all the special mental disabilities that hamper educational progress, the most frequent is a weakness in what may be termed long term memory. Slow learners need to go over material more times before it is fixed in their minds. The efficiency of initial learning is important as well as actual retention and recall; these are all influenced by attitudes, interests and emotional states. But slow learners are unable to retain information in memory storage for a long time and recall the information when it is needed. One of the causes of poor memory in slow learners is weakness in attention.

One way in which remembering can be improved is by ensuring that as many useful associations are made as possible for meaningful associations are of great importance for slow learners for accurate perceptions of the concept. A clear perception is the pathway to better memory. Perception is the cognitive process that identifies, organises and translates sensory data into meaningful information. The product of perception is figural information which is a direct representation of the physical and observable characteristics of our experiences, that is, inferences about how things feel, smell and taste. Meaning is distributed to figural information only when it is associated with environmental events and contents. Perceptual processes include discrimination, co-ordination and sequencing. Discrimination allows us to differentiate among distinctive features within the sensory system, coordination allows the integration of information from two or more information sources, and sequencing enables us to recognise spatial and temporal stimulus sequences and patterns. But the slow learners experience difficulties in these areas of perceptual processing.

c) Distraction and Lack of Concentration

Research works of Curtis, K. and Shaver, J.P. (1980) reveal that the attention span of the slow learners is relatively short. Also, they lack concentration. They can not concentrate on the instruction of the teacher which is mostly verbal exposition for more than thirty minutes at a stretch. They need short and frequent lessons for better perceptions. Modular approach or personalised system of instruction can cater to the needs of slow learners. Media application in the instructional process can draw and sustain their attention for a little longer time and promote concentration also. To overcome distractibility and to promote concentration, multimedia instructional strategy will be very suitable for slow learners. Research studies [Soundararaja Rao and Rajaguru, 1995] reveal that when the learning materials are presented through concrete situations, the slow learners's attention and concentration do not differ significantly from that of a normal student. They are able to concentrate on enjoyable and successful work for a considerable time. The degree to which the work is suited to the slow learners's capacity, and engages interest and activity is important. The slow learner's physical condition and his expectations of success or failure are also influential. In addition, the ability to concentrate seems to be, to some extent, a product of experience and training. Creative and practical activities seem to promote the development of good attention and of work habits.

d) Inability to Express Ideas

Tansley and Gulliford (1962) state that schools give considerable thought to the ways of achieving good standards in reading and writing, but important as reading and writing are it must not be forgotten that they are only subsidiary skills in language, Children's ability to express themselves orally and to comprehend what is said to them is more important. This is where the slow learners are lacking. Slow learners have difficulty in finding and combining words, their immaturity and emotional reluctance being one of the chief reasons for their backwardness in expression. They often have recourse to gestures or to action rather than words.

With slow learners the difficulties are in knowing what to say, or if they know what to say in finding ways of saying it. A small vocabulary is one of the chief weaknesses. The lack of a word or the frequent inability to call it up when needed, results in hesitations, new starts and round about ways of saying things. Expression is often lacking in order, sequence and selectivity. The difficulty in knowing what to select to say is a common enough weakness in expression. Also, the errors in the language usage of the slow learners are, of course, frequent. This can be attributed to the fact that what the slow learner hears out of school is in continual opposition to what he hears in school. He lacks imagination and foresight. He is not able to foresee the consequences in the future. To express ideas one must be good at communication which involves listening as well as talking. But, slow learners are poor at remembering messages and listening to instructions. As a result, they are unable to express ideas with clarity.

CAUSES OF SLOW LEARNING

Even though there are various causative factors for slow learning, only some important ones are discussed below. An insight into the causative factors of slow learning will enable the teachers to identify and combat slow learning at early stage itself. The earlier they are identified, the sooner remedial instruction can be imparted. It is not that all the factors are at work in case of all the slow learners. One or more factors or the interaction between these factors may cause slow learning in case of each slow learner. The following are the prominent causative factors.

a) Poverty

Poverty happens to be the primary factor causing slow learning in a developing country like India. Poverty affects children in two ways (I) by impairing student's health and (ii) by reducing their learning capacity. Poverty produces many mental and moral deprivations which ultimately speak upon the performance of students. "A sound mind in a sound body" is a tenet, Only when the body is sound, the mind can work to its capacity. Our brains can remain sharp and alert, ready for any sort of information processing, only when we have good health which is usually affected by poverty. Poverty affects physical as well as mental health and this leads to intellectual dullness. Wealth plays a prominent role in acquiring general knowledge through enriched experience.

A child from a sophisticated family has a variety of avenues to explore and he gets enough materials to meet his requirements. He gets education, toys and books which are congenial to acquire general knowledge to improve his educational background. Thus his mind is slowly conditioned and trained up to increase his learning rate over the years. On the contrary a child from an impoverished family does not get enough opportunity to live a full life. Since the poor students have no access to such avenues it is not possible for them to sharpen their brain or to increase their learning rate at early stage. Poverty in itself does not necessarily cause slow learning but may create conditions and susceptibilities which may facilitate the onset of slow learning. However, poverty is not the sole cause of slow learning. We have to investigate into other causes to gain first hand knowledge about slow learners.

b) Intelligence of Family Members

Another potent factor that influences the learning of an individual is the level of intelligence of his parents as well as family members. It has its own impact on the learning of children. The educated parents are very keen on the intellectual development of their children. They start teaching and training their children before they are admitted to K.G. Classes. Also, they are able to provide the children with educational toys and books which all facilitate the learning of the children. Further, they themselves do intensive parent tutoring in reading and arithmetic. In this manner they train up their children to increase the learning rate. It is true that educated and intelligent parents can provide educational experiences and materials to their children according to their own intellectual level.

But if the parents are not intelligent or sophisticated, they can not take positive steps towards upliftment of their children. They seldom evince interest in the intellectual development of their children. Neither learning material nor parent tutoring is provided to the children of illiterate parents. As a result, the children of impoverished families do not get adequate opportunities to train up their minds in order to increase their rate of learning. Without knowing arithmetic or alphabets they enter L.K.G. or First standard, whatever the case may be. Such children, when they come to school for the first time, see others far ahead of them and it gives them an inferiority complex which culminates in losing self- confidence. These ultimately lead them to intellectual dullness which facilitates onset of slow learning. Children coming from affluent families which have high socio-economic status are not usually slow learners. Most of the slow learners are from indigent families. Research evidences also confirm this fact.

c) Emotional Factors

All students are likely to have emotional problems at some point in their school career. The slow learners have such serious and long lasting emotional problems that these hamper very much their learning process. These emotional problems of slow learners result in poor academic achievement, poor interpersonal relationship, and poor self-esteem. An important area for personal, social and emotional development for children is self-concept or self-esteem. This aspect of their development will be strongly influenced by experiences at home, with peers, and at school. Self concept includes the way we perceive our strengths, weaknesses, abilities, attitudes and values. Its developments begin at birth and is continually shaped by experience. Lack of positive self-concept can severely damage a child's social development.

Emotional factors contribute a lot towards the slow learning of children. Psychologists have confirmed this through various research findings. When a child comes to school, he brings his emotional world with him. Tension and conflict that the child experiences exercise a negative influence on learning. So, the tensions at home, the relationship between the siblings and parents themselves have an adverse effect on the learning of children, not to mention the frustration which he sustains from his family and the external world. In autocratic homes the children develop fear and frustration which hinder effective learning. Fear and anxiety generated by the teacher's attitude also will emotionally disturb the children. When the children are emotionally upset, tension and frustration set in which cause onset of slow learning.

d) Personal Factors

Besides all the aforesaid factors, there are some personal factors which are also responsible for slow learning. Physical deformities, pathological body conditions, and defects in sight, hearing and speech may pave the way for slow learning. These develop complex in children which adversely affects their learning. Personal factors include long illness or long absence from school and lack of confidence in self. Naturally when they remain absent from school for a long period due to illness or some other reason, they can not keep pace with their classmates and they will lag behind. This will ultimately affect their self confidence and create conditions and susceptibilities which may facilitate the onset of slow learning. It has been pointed out that children, who lack self confidence are slow learners.

Slow learning caused by physical attributes can be easily provided diagnosis and remedial measures are made at early stage itself. It is needless to say that is earlier the better. A careful examination of eyes, ears, throat, speech organs and the central nervous system is very essential. Services of consultants, Paediatricians, opthalmologists, audiologists, neurologists and speech therapists should be effectively made use of. There are children with visual defects other than loss of acuity. There are some hearing defects which may only be revealed by audiometric examination. Similarly, brain damage can not be confirmed without a neurological examination or electro-encephalography. It is not only better but also cheaper to diagnose these defects in early stage itself so that clinical remedy can be ensured before the defects become worse and cause other consequences. There are also children whose physical development and muscular co-ordination are so retarded that they need immediate remedial measures. There are also some others who are malnourished because either feeding is poor or the metabolic processes are faulty. The slow learning problem of such children can be surmounted by ensuring special diet and treatment by nutrition experts.

IDENTIFYING SLOW LEARNERS

Children of to-day are the citizens of tomorrow; they are going to be the pillars of the country. Hence it is essential to ensure that each pillar is as strong as the other. Moreover, we cannot bring about optimum human resource development without uplifting the slow learners who constitute about 18% of the total student population. There is every possibility that each classroom has some slow learners. It is more true so at primary and high school levels. They come to school regularly; but they are likely to become drop-outs if their needs are not adequately met. From psychological point of view, it would be more beneficial to identify the slow learners as early as possible. The earlier they are identified, the sooner they can be subjected to remedial instruction.

From the survey works conducted so far it is observed that it is somehow easier to identify more severely handicapped children than the mildly handicapped ones. But, a teaching expert can easily make out any deviation in the classroom behaviour pertaining to learning difficulties of children. The teacher is the right person, by virtue of his position and his frequent interaction with the students, to adjudge the learning rate of his students. Manifestation of certain drawbacks and learning difficulties will naturally draw the attention of the teacher towards such slow learning children. Also, the teacher has primary knowledge about the fact which spells out clearly that the slow learners require more time and more help to acquire the predetermined skills than the average children. Hence, the earlier we identify the slow learners; the better we can combat slow learning.

NEED FOR EARLY IDENTIFICATION

Early identification and prevention are basic goals of intervention programmes for any category of problem or backward students. For slow learners these goals present peculiar difficulties, yet it is not without promise. The difficulties are related to identifying the specific causes of slow learning, the particular promise is that the slow learners so much respond to special remedial instruction that preventive efforts and remedial measures seem to have a chance of success. Because children's behaviour is quite responsive to conditions in the social environment and can be shaped by adults, the potential for primary prevention preventing serious behaviour problems from occurring in the first place - would seem to be great.

If the slow learning is due to the specific cause of emotional disturbance of the child, an early identification and required intervention will be very fruitful. Research evidences also confirm this. Early intervention with preschoolers, whether they are aggressive or withdrawn, has the potential to make many such children 'normal' - that is, indistinguishable from their peers - by the time they are in the elementary grades. Slow learning caused by physical attributes can be easily overcome if the problem is identified at early stage before it becomes worse or leads to complication. There are some students who stand out as being obviously extremely backward due to poor physical co-ordination, their clumsy manipulation, and their very retarded speech. When these physical attributes are set right, slow learning can be tackled by providing physiotherapy and proper training. Identifying and intervening at early stage will be more feasible and fruitful. Though the slow learners come to school regularly they are likely to become drop outs if their needs are not adequately met. Only earlier identification can ensure effective intervention which will diminish wastage and stagnation to a considerable extent. From psychological point of view also it would be better to identify the slow learners earlier. All these arguments stress the importance of identifying the slow learners at an early stage and also the operating causative factors so that required remedial measures can be taken up not only to alleviate the causative factor but also to ameliorate their learning process. The earlier, the better is the golden rule here.

A THREE PHASE PROCESS

Psychologists and educationists have devised various tools and techniques to identify slow learners. Tansley and Gulliford (1962) have laid down four different measures whereas Chintamani Kar (1992) has propogated seven measures to identify slow learners. But identifying the slow learners on the basis of a three phase process will be more feasible and more reliable. The three phases are:

i) Initial Identifying phase
ii) Scientific confirmatory phase
iii) Counter - check phase

i) Initial Identifying Phases

To identify the slow learners initially the following techniques are very useful.

(a) Observation Technique
(b) An Educational Assessment
(c) A Social History of the Child in his family and Cultural Setting.

The aforesaid three techniques can be used separately or in any mode of combination to identify the slow learners. The speciality of these techniques is that the teacher does not require any testing tool to identify the slow learners.

On the contrary, he can easily identify the slow learners by means of his careful observation of the child. Also, a critical educational assessment of the child and knowing the social history of the child can easily bring the slow learners into the focus of the teacher. Since all the records required for making an educational assessment of the child are at the disposal, the teacher can easily complement the findings of his observation with educational assessment of the child. A deep insight into each technique is essential for properly identifying the slow learners.

a) Observation Technique

This is the most convenient and practically the foremost technique to identify slow learners. Observation of children's behaviour by the teacher as well as experts helps in identifying slow learners. This can be done under simple as well as controllable conditions. While making observation of the children's behaviour, a strict vigil should be kept to study their reactions to various situations. A child's behaviour can be observed not only in the classroom, but also on the playground, home and in the group. Observation can be done by just scrupulously watching the child at close quarters and by moving along with the child. How he grasps the instructional presentation, how he responds in the classroom and in the school premises should be noted down and analysed properly. It should be kept in mind that the observer should have the capacity for analysing and interpreting the information he gets from his observation. Observation technique is very congenial for ascertaining the curricular, co-curricular, extra-curricular and recreational interest of the children. In educational programmes such as recitation of a memory poem or reproduction of an essay or passage or testing comprehension, observation can easily bring to light the slow learners. But observation technique alone will not suffice for reliable identification for there is a possible chance to confuse an under-achiever with a slow learner. So, there is a need to complement observation technique with other technique or techniques.

b) An Educational Assessment

An educational assessment provides a detailed description of the child in the school setting, giving information about:

1. The child's level of attainment in the basic subjects in terms of what he can do, what his special difficulties appear to be, and what steps have already been tried, e.g. whether remedial measures have been attempted, and if so, by what method and with what result. Evaluation of deficiencies in

school achievement is possible through scholastic tests. These tests can throw light on areas like arithmetic, reading, spelling, composition, writing language and comprehension. General and specific problems of children can be easily singled out by the psychologists and the teachers through scholastic tests, and causes of anomalies can also be evaluated properly.

2. The child's level of language development and speech - Slow learners are usually found to be wanting in this respect.
3. Standards of achievement in other areas of curriculum, e.g. in art, practical subjects, physical education.
4. Emotional and social behaviour as displayed both in and out of the classroom.
5. Interest in and attitude towards school.
6. Previous school history with particular reference to attitude towards school, changes of school and regularity of attendance.
7. The child's interest and background knowledge.
8. Degree of parental co-operation - Lack of parental co-operation has been found to facilitate the onset of slow learning.

All the above measures can be undertaken by the teacher with the records available at his disposal. These bring to light not only the slow learning of the children but also signify the causes for that.

c) A Social History of the Child in his Family and Cultural Setting

Most discussions about backward children lead to the point when the importance of the home as a powerful factor in the child's response to school is agreed upon. Efforts should be made to find out about birth conditions, age of passing the 'milestones', stages in speech development, illness and accidents and any marked irregularities in development. Details about the family history, particularly with reference to mental or physical illnesses that may have a bearing on the child's condition and the facts about the cultural and economic factors in the home should also be gathered and noted down. Then family attitudes and relationships should be assessed. This is a most important aspect to assess, for the emotional climate of the home, the attitude towards the child, and the way difficulties in development have been met can be powerful determinants of the child's capacity to learn. The aforesaid three techniques used sequentially or simultaneously will enable the teacher to identify the slow learners more reliably.

ii) Scientific Confirmatory Phase

The slow learners identified in the first phase should be subjected to certain scientific confirmatory tests for better reliability and accuracy. Further, these rests helps the teacher to discriminate between the slow learners and other backward children like under achievers. Many standardised tests which can be administered as scientific confirmatory tests are now available.

They are:

a) Terman - Merrill Scale
b) Wechsler - Intelligence Scale
c) Other Intelligence tests in Common Use
d) Ravens Progressive matrices
e) Personality Test
f) Psychometric and psychological Test
g) Medical Examination

Administering one or more than one of the above tests to the identified slow learners we can easily confirm whether we have correctly identified the slow learners. These tests will be very useful to differentiate a slow learner from other backward children as stated earlier. A thorough knowledge of these tests is essential for those who are entrusted with the task of instructing the slow learners. A detailed description of how these tests can be used to identify slow learners can be found in Slow Learners: Their psychology and Instruction (Reddy, Ramar, Kusuma, 1997).

iii) Countercheck phase

The slow learners identified and then confirmed by scientific confirmatory test can be once again counter-checked either on the basis of rate of learning as suggested by Kirk (1962) or on the basis of Sandra's Checklist as recommended by Chintamani Kar (1992)

COUNTERCHECK BY RATE OF LEARNING

Kirk (1962, 1971) took rate of learning as the basis for identifying slow learners. According to him, the slow learners, gifted and the average children can be classified according to their rate of learning. In 1968 Bloom proposed that rather than providing all students with the same amount of instructional time and allowing learning to differ, perhaps we should require that all or almost all students reach certain level of achievement by allowing time to differ. That is, Bloom suggests that we give students as much time and instruction as necessary to bring them all to a reasonable level of learning. Suppose we expect 80 percent mastery level. Then we can assess learning rate in the following manner.

A specific passage from science or social science may be taught by the teacher. Then the students may be instructed to make a thorough study of passage. To ascertain their mastery, some 20 to 25 objective type test items can be framed based on the passage dealt with. Then the teacher should note down how much time each student takes to get 80 percent score. The time taken by each student to attain 80% mastery level will signify his rate of learning. Naturally slow learners will take more time to attain the specified mastery level than average and gifted students.

EDUCATIONAL PROGRAMMES FOR SLOW LEARNERS

Psychologists and educationists have recommended various educational programmes to surmount the problem of slow learners in the mainstreaming. Most of the measures are within the purview of the teachers. Effectiveness of certain measures have already been established by the researchers,. A clear perception of the educational programmes meant for slow learners will enable the teacher to combat slow learning in an effective manner. The following are the remedial measures which constitute the educational programmes for slow learners.

i. Motivation
ii. Individual Attention
iii. Restoration and Development of Self-confidence
iv. Development of Good Work Habits
v. Elastic Curriculum
vi. Remedial Instruction1
vii. Healthy Environment
viii. Periodical Medical Check-up
ix. Special Methods of Teaching
x. Learning Contracts and Peer Tutoring.

i) Motivation

Experience has shown us that learning failure is very often largely due to poor motivation. Children taught by a teacher using motives in a sensible, individualised way will always learn more quickly and better, even if the method used to learn is faulty. Slow learners usually evince an attitude of avoidance resulting from previous experience of failure or dislike of a subject. They often glance at words rather than scrutinize them carefully, with the result that their errors in recall are the result of guessing from slight clues such as initial letters or superficial similarities. Fear of failure and disinterest are evident in their daily school activities. It emphasises the need to take adequate and appropriate measures to improve their academic status. When a light improvement is noticed, the teacher should not fail to employ some effective motivational techniques to stimulate the slow learners. But in day-to-day classroom practice, most of the teachers go about their work in a routine manner without caring for the children in general and backward children in particular and apathetically carry on the classroom work, accomplishing very little. This leads to large scale wastage of human resource in terms of human potentiality.

The key to avert this state of affairs lies in motivations, that is why motivation is rightly said to be the royal road to success. An encouraging smile from the teacher can do better than his verbal instruction. When the teacher succeeds in motivating the students, his instruction will be effective and the educational objectives can be achieved. The teacher should be wary not to discourage the slow learners who usually feel frustrated. The teacher should let them understand that they are not the ignored students and they are as dear to him as others are. When the teacher evinces this type of positive attitude, all his motivational techniques will work out successfully. Moreover, motivation not only instigates the behaviour of slow learners but also reinforces the on-going behaviour. In the classroom situation motivation is that which drives the slow learners to learn. It makes the slow learners desirous of learning to apply himself to the tasks. In addition to encouraging smile and kind verbal motivation, the teacher can make use of appropriate illustration, example and aids for creating motivational atmosphere inside the class.

ii) Individual Attention

"Individual attention" refers to the attention given by the teacher to a particular student. Of all the students it is the slow learners who need individual attention from the teacher. The individual differences of the children should be properly recognised and the individuality of the child must be respected. The teacher should take positive effort to ascertain the specific disability of the slow learners and accordingly he should devise his remedial instructional strategy which should cater to needs of each slow learner. It is necessary that the handling teachers should be very kind and sympathetic towards slow learners.

Bloom 91976) advocates mastery learning strategy for backward students wherein he allows time to vary for mastery. As we have official special coaching classes for the scheduled caste and scheduled tribes students studying in the schools for which the expenditure is borne by the state, we can have similar type of special classes for the slow learners in the evening after school hours so that they can be given more time as well as better individual attention. Some incentives may be provided to those teachers who may be entrusted with the task of instructing the slow learners in the way the government gives incentives for those teachers who take special coaching classes for the SC/ ST students. If this remedial measure is enforced, better individual attention can be given to the slow learners in the special classes which will, ultimately, promote better human resource development.

iii) Restoration and Development of Self-Confidence

Slow learners are the backward children who have, even before admission to the school, experienced years of failure and frustration as a result of which their self-esteem is seriously undermined. Constant lack of academic success, rejection by other children, faulty instruction and mismanagement by parents lead to emotional disturbance, feelings of inadequacy and personality and conduct disorders. These slow learners ultimately find themselves in a vicious circle. The interplay between the causes and symptoms becomes more and more complicated and difficult to disentangle. The breaking of this vicious circle becomes one of the most important objectives of remedial treatment. This cannot be broken unless the school establishes a special educational programme for the slow learners.

The teacher should instill self confidence in the minds of slow learners. For that he should avoid magnifying the mistakes committed by the slow learners. He should also avert all sorts of sarcastic censure. He should manifest a sympathetic attitude towards slow learners. When the slow learners find themselves in some difficulties, the teacher should guide them properly. When they are right or when they give a right response, the teacher should effectively make use of that opportunity to praise the concerned slow learner for his correct response. This type of praise, as well as encouragement, will imbibe self confidence in slow learners and they can make remarkable progress and increase their learning capacity in course of time. So the teacher should take all possible effort and make use of all possible opportunities to restore and develop self-confidence in slow learners and they can make use of all possible opportunities to restore and develop self-confidence in slow learners which will ultimately goad them into manifesting better attainment. Nothing succeeds like success and success leads to success.

iv) Development of Good Work Habits

Backwardness of slow learning children is often the result of development of poor attitude towards work. Work that is too difficult or beyond the entering behaviour of the slow learners usually results in boredom and poor attention. Frequent failures and frustration may cause behaviour difficulties and reluctance to try or to take initiative. If careful attention is given to individualisation of treatment, curriculum content and balance and to suitable organisation, the slow learners can develop the feeling of power to overcome difficulties and improve in self-directed application to work. Moreover, the slow learners lack the knack to assess the relative importance of work. They not only do not know how to do a work but also when to do a work and which to do first. They may be doing a work at wrong time which will eventually retard learning.

So it becomes an essential duty of the teacher to develop good work habits in slow learners. How to study each subject, how to tackle the problems related to the subject and how to make responses for the questions and how to carry out the project or enrichment activities should be well explained to slow learners and a strict vigil also should be kept to make sure that they follow the guidelines given by the teacher in learning the subject. It should be made known to them how approach and instructional strategy differ from subject to subject and how they should tackle each subject. They should be instructed to adapt systematic study habits at home also. If the work habits of the slow learners are developed as stated above, they will be able to attain a moderate degree of success within a considerable period of time.

v) Elastic Curriculum

Utmost care should be taken in preparing the curriculum for the slow learners which should be as flexible as possible to suit the requirement and need of the individual slow learners who are generally interested in concrete perceptual experiences. So greater attention must be paid towards concrete aspects of work. The teachers should not lay much stress on abstract and theoretical study because the slow learners cannot understand the abstract concepts very easily. Wherever there are abstract concepts, the teacher should try to establish possible relationship or point out possible associations so that the slow learners can have a grasp of the abstract concepts. There must be scope for profuse use of audio-visual aids and for concrete presentation of subject content. When there is concrete presentation of instructional content, the slow learners are able to understand in a better way and it enhances their learning capacity and learning rate to a considerable extent.

Practical work should be given due importance in the curriculum of the slow learners. In the mainstreaming also we have crafts, arts etc which provide for practical work and work experience. The four purposes of education i.e. self realisation, human relationship, economic efficiency and civic responsibility can be developed in slow learners by incorporating proper practical work and work experience in the curriculum. Practical work is one of the several fields in which the slow learners can often most easily achieve success or have it engineered for them. The work done must therefore be suited to the capacity of individual children; it should be something which produces evidence of success by looking good or being useful. In the early stages at least, slow learners need quick success; they can not be expected to persist for too long without tangible results. It is to be remembered here that learning builds on learning in the way success builds on success.

The practical works which are found to be conducive to slow learners include metal work, wood work, leather work, cane work, knitting, tailoring and other subjects of household economy. There is, too, a great deal of useful knowledge that comes through practical work, the names and uses of different woods, materials, tools and processes. There is the learning about how things are made; where materials come from; how much materials and tools cost; measurement and the appreciation of size and quantity. Wherever possible, opportunities should be taken to use interest in the craft as a starting point for the incidental discovery of more knowledge and understanding of the world around.

Physical education must not be solely concerned with the development of strength and physical skills, or indeed with physical development alone. It should be viewed as an integral part of the whole programme for personality development. It should include, at all levels, training in personal hygiene and general fitness, and the development of co-operation, courage and confidence, perseverance and independence. It should provide opportunities for exploration and experiment in the use physical activity and the use of skill and strength in work and play. Because of their poor home environments, or as a result of rejection, slow learners have missed the opportunities for skill learning which arise naturally in play. It should be noted that the adverse effects of these missed opportunities are cumulative. Primary skills are not developed and consequently more mature ones are harder to learn. This may lead to further rejection and isolation. Physical education should take into account and help to minimise those physical limitations which occur most frequently in slow learners - poor posture and muscular incoordination, lack of stamina, specific physical defects. Finally, physical education should take advantage of the many opportunities it will have to compensate for other limitation and to ensure feelings of accomplishment and success. So the subject teachers should refrain from engaging the physical education periods for their own subjects.

vi) Remedial Instruction

Educators have suggested that the remedial teaching classes or special classes should be conducted systematically based on laid down guidelines. Studies have proved the effectiveness of remedial classes in case of specific slowness in a specific subject area. First, the deficiencies are determined and confirmed by experts administering some diagnostic tests to slow learners. Then the expertise of specialists may be utilised to deal with specific slowness. The following are the guidelines for the smooth working of a remedial programme.

(a) The instructional content must be very carefully graded keeping in mind the capacity, requirement, educational and experience levels of the students. In the gradation of teaching materials the principles of proceeding from easy to difficult and simple to complex must be scrupulously followed.

(b) Short frequent lessons should be introduced instead of long lessons every week. This will cater to the short span of attention of slow learners. Further, it will avert fatigue and boredom, to which the slow learners are easily susceptible.

(c) The slow learners are able to grasp concrete ideas rather than abstract ideas. Therefore there must be ample use of audio visual aids in the instructional process which can provide unique experience to the slow learners in the presentation of the content. Concrete presentation of instructional content can be made by making use of appropriate media application in the instructional process.

(d) The teacher should be aware of the fact that a friendly approach in remedial teaching is highly conducive. Friendly smile, a few encouraging words, praise at appropriate time will have a far reaching influence on the learning capacity of slow learners. The cumulative effects of these procedures will make better impact on the achievement of slow learners than even an effective instruction.

(e) To generate interest, social skills and confidence in slow learners, stress may be laid on effective use of art, music and drama. These are certain areas where they can have a moderate success which imbibes in them self confidence. Moreover, nothing succeeds like success; and success builds on success.

(f) The teachers dealing with the slow learners should give due importance to practice, drill and review which all facilitate the comprehension and retention of slow learners. Repetition and revision should also be emphasised. For this computer assisted instruction and modular instruction can be made use of since these teaching strategies effectively incorporate practice, drill review, revision and repetition in the instructional process.

With a view to ensure optimum human resource development special remedial classes should be arranged for slow learners. When we provide extra time for slow learners for corrective instruction, they also can achieve the mastery level. As we have special coaching classes for the SC/ST students in the evening hours, we can have special remedial classes for the slow learners also. In case of SC/ST special coaching classes, four teachers for tackling the boys of Stds VIII to X and eight teachers handling students of Stds XI and XII are paid by the state. In similar manner, the teachers entrusted with the task of remedial coaching for slow learners also can be paid by the state with a view to optimise human resource development.

vii) Healthy Environment

Providing a healthy environment is an important aspect of remedial measures for slow learners. The school environment should be healthy and reasonably free for slow learners. Many a time poor environmental factors contribute a lot towards the slowness. Poor environmental factors should be adequately tackled or removed at the earliest so that congenial atmosphere can be created for the effective learning of slow learners. Again, the teachers should ensure a variety of approaches in the instructional presentation to teach various subjects. Most often slow learners suffer from emotional problems. So utmost care must be taken to place them in protected environment. To ensure this, the teacher himself should not criticise the slow learners nor should he allow the other students either to look down upon the slow learners or to tease them. When they have no emotional problems, their learning will be optimum.

viii) Periodical Medical Check-up

Physical anomalies sometimes serve as vital contributory factors for slow learning. Poor health and other malfunctions also have adverse effect on the learning of slow learners. If a particular anomaly is detected and correctly diagnosed, then a slow learner can become a normal learner after remedial treatment. In absence of periodical medical check-up, there will be no opportunity for the teacher to diagnose the cause of slow learning and to ensure the possible medical remedy. Moreover, for every physical malady there is a medical remedy which can remedy not only the malady but also the slow learning. So special medical check-up should be arranged periodically for every slow learner.

ix) Special Methods of Teaching

Educationists have conducted many experiments to evolve special method of teaching for slow learners. Rajaguru (1994) has proved the effectiveness of video instruction with special reference to slow learners. Ramar (1996), Reddy and Ramar (1994, 1995, 1997) have highlighted the impact of multimedia based modular approach on the achievement of slow learners.

The research evidences reveal that the following special methods will be very effective for slow learners.

a. Audio and Video Instruction
b. Mastery Learning Strategy with Extra Corrective Instruction
c. Modular Instruction
d. Computer Assisted Instruction.

It is not necessary here to delve into the details of each of the above instructional strategies. But it is very necessary to know how each of the above strategies is effective to slow learners and how far they help the slow learners to overcome their problems. Teachers teaching slow learners can use any single method or a combination of methods in any mode to ensure attainment of mastery level or predeterminded behavioural objectives.

a) Audio and video Instruction

Slow learners need extra time for remedial and enrichment activities. In the audio instruction the expert's service not ordinarily available in the school is made available. They can listen to the audio instruction based on their subject units in the evening hours. They can take them home and make use of according to their convenience. Here the acquisition of informations takes place without any sort of inhibition. Also, they can listen to relevant educational radio programme which also has positive effect on the slow learner's learning.

Video instruction provides for considerable visualisation of objects and processes which is very essential for better perception of concept. What impact a visual presentation can do, any amount of verbal exposition can not do. Moreover, in a fast developing world where knowledge explosion is taking place in every sphere, it is unreasonable, to expect that written or spoken words alone could convey the volume of relevant information to the learner. Further, the video instruction provides unique experience to the slow learners in the presentation of instructional content. It penetrates more deeply into human character with an immediate excitement than any other single medium. Concrete presentation of instructional content ensured in Video instruction is very conducive for the slow learner for making a better perception of the concept. The dual effect of audio and video strengthens and enriches the understanding and expedites the mastery of the concept.

Video instructional strategy very much caters to the individual differences of slow learners. In the traditional classroom settings, the slow learners are too inhibited to ask the teacher to clarify a concept or to get a doubt cleared. But, in the video instructional strategy, even if they don't understand the concept at the first attempt, they can understand the concept thoroughly by making use of the provisions such as 'pause', 'still', and 'play back'. Not only that, but also they can take the video cassettes to their houses and view the instructional programme according to their convenience. This enables the slow learners to learn better at their own rate.

b) Mastery Learning Strategy

One widely used means of adapting instruction to the needs of diverse students is called mastery learning. Mastery learning is a system of instruction that emphasises the achievement of instructional objectives by all students by allowing learning time to vary. The basic idea behind mastery learning is to make sure that all or almost all the students have learned a particular skill to a pre-established level of mastery before moving on to the next skill.

Bloom (1976) proposes that 80 percent of the students should be able to achieve at a level usually attained by only 20 percent of students when they are given additional time and that under these circumstances aptitude or ability should be nearly unrelated to achievement. Mastery learning emphasises corrective instructions in the form of remedial special classes in the evening hours. Given some extra coaching and corrective instruction, slow learners are able to make a better achievement. Corrective instruction refers to educational activities given to students who initially fail to master an objective.

This mastery learning strategy does not involve any expenditure. All that we need is an understanding dedicated teacher who can devotedly tackle the slow learners. Corrective instruction can be imparted in the remedial special classes in the evening hours. The teacher should give them some freedom and at the same time the progress of the slow learners should be monitored and guided. Peer tutoring can also be effectively made use of wherever possible. Services of aides, special education teachers, parent volunteers can also be used in remedial special classes of slow learners. For mastery learning media application, and individualised instruction also will be very conducive for slow learners. Once the slow learners have the experience of mastery learning and attain a pre-determined mastery level, the learning will build on learning leading them to a remarkable success or achievement.

c) Modular Instruction

Module is a self contained auto instructional package dealing with a single conceptual unit or subject matter. Instruction through modules has been found very effective for all levels of students and it is found more effective with regard to low achievers and slow learners. Various research evidences confirm this (Ramar (1996); Reddy and Ramar 1994, 1995,1996, 1997). This modular instruction as a special method of teaching can be very effective to slow learners since it enables the slow learners to adequately overcome their problems in learning. A detailed account of how each of the problems of slow learners is overcome in the modular instruction can be systematically listed out.

The slow learners lack concentration. So they can not concentrate on the instructional presentation for more than 45 minutes. In modular instruction a single unit is divided into three to four conceptual sub units. Each sub unit constitutes the subject content for development of one module. The duration of each module is 20 to 25 minutes only. So the slow learners will be able to concentrate on the concept. Also, it caters to the short span of attention of the slow learners.

A learning module is a self contained and self instructional package dealing with a single conceptual unit or subject matter. It can be used in any setting, convenient to the learner and the learner can complete the module at his own pace. It may be used individually or in small learning groups. In this way modular instruction accommodates instruction to individual differences. Here, what matters most is the mastery of the subject, not the time. So the modules are very suitable to the students and they are more effective for slow learners.

One of the most frequent complaints about slow learners is the weakness of their memory. Of all the problems that hamper educational progress, the most frequent is a weakness in what may be termed long-term memory. Slow learners need to go over the material more times before it is fixed in their mind, and more frequent revision is required to prevent forgetting. The efficiency of the initial learning is important as well as actual retention and recall. Modular instruction takes care of these problems by providing frequent revision and repetition in each module.

The slow learners are very poor in abstract thinking. It is because they are unable to understand the relationship between things. They are slower to perceive and use possible association. Meaningful associations are of great importance not only for comprehension but also for prolonged retention. The learning materials presented in the module for each objective the project work and the practicum incorporated in the learning module enable the slow learners to surmount the problem of abstract thinking and to understand the possible association which will, ultimately, tell upon their retention.

It is fallacy to think that just because slow learners are limited in intelligence, they can only learn by rote memorisation. They also can make meaningful learning where there is concrete presentation of subject matter. Slow learners must understand as much as they can of what they are learning; and then they need more repetition, revision and practice to ensure retention. Modular instruction takes care of concrete presentation of subject matter by incorporating necessary diagrams, sketches, pictures, worksheets, examples, dimensional drawings etc, with the learning material at appropriate places. Also, modular instruction provides for the required review, repetition, and revision by highlighting the main points in learning materials, various tests and in recapitulation and summary. It provides for practice in project work and practicum. Thus, in many ways, the modular instruction proves to be suitable for slow learners.

d) Computer Assisted Instruction

Computer assisted instruction is a kind of individualised instruction administered by a computer. The computers that are programmed to guide students through lessons at a student's own pace can help in accomodating student differences. Computer assisted instruction has its roots in programmed instruction and in the behavioural theories of learning. According to these theories, learning is accelerated by the use of controlled presentation of stimuli, followed by reinforcement based upon the learner's responses. Many CAI programmes stress drill and practice exercises, others teach students facts and concepts. CAI programmes have the following advantages.

1. Use of a structured curriculum
2. Letting students work at their own pace.
3. Giving students controlled, frequent feed-back and reinforcement.
4. Measuring performance quickly and giving students information on their performance.

Therefore, for the slow learners, who remain in the lowest rung of the ladder, CAI is reckoned as one of the most suitable strategies which can motivate them to manifest their best. Why and how far the CAI is conducive to slow learners can be listed as below.

CAI provides unique experience to the learners in respect of the presentation of the content. It ensures easy and effective transmission of instruction to the learners. It gives instant knowledge of results and provides immediate feed back which are very essential for slow learners to ameliorate their learning process.

It effectively caters to individual differences. Every student can learn at his own rate. Students will have no pinch of inhibition when they learn through CAI. The feeling that they are not preyed upon the supervisors and the free and relaxed readiness to learn by themselves at their own rates, give the slow learners an impetus to learn better and to manifest their best.

In case of teaching science through CAI programme, important diagrams can be magnified even part by part also, so that the slow learners can understand in a better way. Moreover, the simulation technique which is possible in a CAI programme will also facilitate learning of slow learners.

It is not that the aforesaid special methods are the only methods to improve the learning capacity of the slow learners. The teacher can use any other method also according to situation and feasibility to teach the slow learners. Since the effectiveness of the above methods with reference to backward students has been confirmed by research evidences, they have been highlighted here. But the teacher has every right to choose any method of teaching that he deems fit and proper for improving the learning capacity of the slow learners. Here what matters much is development in the learning rate of slow learners, not the method that is employed. Methods are only means to achieve our preestablished behavioural objectives.

X. Learning Contracts and Peer Tutoring

a) Learning Contracts

A Learning contract is an agreement between the teacher and the student to study and share information about a specific topic. It helps the classroom teacher organise the instructional programme for some exceptional students. Dunn and Dunn (1974) describe the contracting process in some detail. They discuss the importance of joint (student teacher) planning of the elements of the contract, and indicate that the contract's behavioural objectives should be personalised. They also suggest that the contract include a list of media or resources and activities the student will use, as well as any methods the student will use to report what has been learned. Finally, they suggest that the contract indicate how the student's performance will be evaluated and, if appropriate, what the schedule will be for completing the project. Contracting may be effective for gifted students or for backward students like under achievers, slow learners etc who are motivated when allowed to participate in designing their instructional activities.

b) Peer Tutoring

Long ago educators realised that students could help one another learn. When one student teaches another, this is called peer tutoring. There are two principal types of peer tutoring; cross-age tutoring where the tutor is several years older than the student being taught and same-age peer tutoring, where one student tutors a classmate. Cross-age tutoring is more often recommended by researchers than same age tutoring, partly because of the obvious fact that older students are more likely to know the material, and partly because students may accept an old student as a tutor but resent having a classmate appointed to tutor them.

When implementing peer tutoring, it is important that the rules for tutors be quite explicit; that is, tutors show or tell their students what to do, then watch as the students perform, they repeat the demonstration or instructions if the student makes an error, and then praise the student when the response is correct. Teacher monitoring of the tutors is an integral part of the system. It is not time consuming, but it is extremely important. Each student must demonstrate mastery of the skill before teaching it, and each should use methods and materials with which the tutor and the teacher have worked previously. Learning tasks to be presented by the tutor should be structured. In every case the tutor should be briefed exactly what the learner should learn and provided with all the necessary materials. Sometimes these materials include task cards with step-by-step instruction, plus concrete materials for completion of task. At other times the materials may be worksheets or book pages, and the task for the learner is to complete the page.

One caution about the research on peer tutoring: Almost all students of peer tutoring use tutoring in addition to regular instruction, and compare results to those for regular instruction alone. For this reason, at least part of the effectiveness of peer tutoring could be attributed to the extra instructional time rather than to the value of peer tutoring itself. However, viewed as an addition to regular classroom instruction, peer tutoring does seem to be an effective way to provide appropriate levels of instruction to students (Slavin, R.E., 1986). This makes it more relevant to slow learners who are in dire need of additional instructional time.

SUMMARY

Slow Learners are those children who are unable to cope with the work normally expected of their age group. Students with IQ 80 to 90 who are traditionally labelled 'dull normal' are generally slow to 'catch on' to whatever is being taught if it involves symbolic, abstract or conceptual subject matter. In the early grades in school, they most often have problems in reading and arithmetic and are labelled slow learners.

Limited cognitive capacity, poor memory distraction and lack of concentration, and inability to express ideas are the important characteristics of slow learners. The causes of slow learning include poverty, intelligence of family members, emotional factors and personal factors.

Slow learners can be identified on the basis of a three-phase process. The three phases are initial identification phase, scientific confirmatory phase and counter-check phase. This three-phase process makes use of both formal and informal measures.

Educational programmes for slow learners include, motivation, individual attention, restoration and development of self-confidence, development of good work habits, elastic curriculum, remedial instruction, healthy environment, periodical medical check-up, special methods of teaching, and learning contracts and peer tutoring.

REFERENCE

Chintamani Kar (1992) *Exceptional Children: Their Psychology and Instruction.* Sterling Publishers Private Limited, New Delhi.

Reddy, G.L., Ramar. R., (1996) *Relative Effectiveness of Video Instruction in Teaching Science and Social Science to Slow Learners.* Paper Presented in the IIIrd National Seminar on Development of Educational Technology, Bharathidasan University, December 27, 1996.

Reddy, G.L., and Ramar, R. (1996) *Identifying Slow Learners.* ICCW Journal, Vol.4, No. 1 and 2, July December 1997.

Reddy G.L., and Ramar. R. (1997) *Effectiveness of Multimedia Instructional Strategy in Teaching, Science to Slow Learners.* Journal of Indian Education, NCERT, Vol. 23, No.2, August 1997.

Reddy, G.L., and Ramar, R. (1997). *Effectiveness of Multimedia Based Modular Approach in Teaching English to Slow Learners.* Journal of disabilities and Impairments, Vol. 11(1), (1997).

Reddy, G.L., and Ramar, R. (1997).*Efficacy of Video Instruction On Achievement of Slow Learners in Mathematics.* Journal of Educational Technology Vol.2, 1997.

Reddy, G.L., Ramar R., and Kusuma, A (1997) *Slow Learners: Their Psychology and Instruction.* Discovery Publishing House, New Delhi.

Slavin, R.E. (1986) *Educational Psychology: theory into Practice.* Prentice hall International Toronto.

Soundararaja Rao and Rajaguru (1995). *Effectiveness Video Assisted Instruction on the Achievement of Slow Learners.* Journal of Educational Research and Extension, Vol.32, No.2, October 1995.

Tansley, A.E., and Gulliford, R. (1962). *The Education of Slow Learning* Children Routeledge Kegan Paul Ltd, London.

6

LEARNING DISABLED CHILDREN

OBJECTIVES

This chapter deals with learning disabled children. The causes of learning disabilities and characteristics of learning disabled children are described. Also, the educational programmes for the learning disabled children are outlined. After reading this chapter, the readers should be able to:

1. Define learning disabilities
2. List out the characteristics of learning disabled children.
3. Understand the causes of learning disabilities.
4. Identify learning disabled children
5. Develop an insight into the intervention programmes for learning disabled children.

The field of learning disabilities is the newest challenging sub-area of the broader field of special education. It was at a parents meeting in New York City in the early 1960s that this term was proposed by Samuel Kirk as a compromise because of the confusing variety of labels that were being used then to describe the child with relatively normal intelligence who was having learning problems. In those days, such a child was likely to be referred to as being minimally brain injured, a slow learner, a dyslexic or perceptually disabled (Hallahan and Kauffman, 1991). Hence this label 'learning disabilities' was most welcome to parents who had anticipated a diagnosis of mental retardation. To those parents who were certain that their child was only unmotivated, it had a traumatic effect. And to the professionals in the field of special education it has a variety of meanings, depending on experience, perspective, or related information about the student in question.

It is learning disabilities that are the most vague and mystifying when compared to other major handicapping or disabling conditions, with the possible exception of emotional disturbances. It is only at a later date that learning disabilities were officially recognised than other handicapping conditions and so there is still a great deal of debate as to what is meant by the term learning disabilities. There are many reasons why the field of learning disabilities is receiving considerable public attention. Persisting hope for remediation characterises the field, stimulated by examples of those unique individuals who purportedly had severe learning disabilities in their youth, yet made significant contributions to society as adults. Individuals such as Thomas Edison, George patton, Woodrow Wilson, Albert Einstein, and many other distinguished men are said to have had a learning disability. Even one of the world's most famous writers of children's literature, Hans Christian Anderson had a severe reading.

In this text, we are taking broad view of learning disabilities, examining their possible causes and a variety of educational techniques and procedures that will be very effective to ameliorate the educational and social progress of the learning disabled. As we explore the field of learning disabilities, a challenging sub-area of the broader field of special education, we are confronted with more questions than answers, more contradictions than accepted facts. It is so because the field is quite new and the group of persons whom we now call learning disabled is unusually diverse. Another continuing problem is the lack of consensus about many major issues. But it is encouraging to observe that the organisation and development of programmes for students with learning disabilities have had a positive effect in the lives of many of those students.

DEFINITIONS OF LEARNING DISABILITIES

The generally recognised date for the first definition of learning disabilities is April 6, 1973 when a parent group called the Fund for Perceptually Handicapped Children was holding its first annual meeting in which a number of recognised advocates and authorities of these students, who were soon to be called learning disabled, were present as speakers, with Samuel Kirk among the more prominent. Kirk (1963) used the term learning disabilities to describe children who had disorders in development in language, speech, reading and associated communication stills needed for social interaction. He also made it clear that he did not include as learning disabled those children whose primary handicap was generalised mental retardation or sensory impairment like blindness or deafness. Parents were so impressed with the potential of this new term ' learning disabilities, that they voted in this same convention, to organise the Association for Children with Learning Disabilities (ACLD). This is how the field of learning disabilities was born which became a very rapidly growing baby. The Association for Children with Learning Disabilities became a powerhouse as advocacy organisation very soon.

It is for administrative convenience and to provide a focal point for advocacy efforts that the term ' learning disabilities' came into being as a conglomerate of conditions grouped under one label. This was much appreciated by most of the parents for they recognised that this was an essential step toward recognition and educational programming for children. The establishment of a National Advisory Committee on Handicapped Children marked the second major event in the evolution of a definition of learning disabilities. The first National Advisory Committee on Handicapped Children was headed by Samuel Kirk. The first annual report of the committee was presented on January 31, 1968. The committee made ten recommendations including a definition. The committee suggested the following definition.

"Children with special learning disabilities exhibit a disorder in one or more of the basic psychological processes involved in understanding or in using spoken or written languages. These may be manifested in disorders of listening, thinking, talking, reading, writing, speaking, or arithmetic. They include conditions, which have been referred to as perceptual handicaps, brain injury, minimal brain dysfunction, dyslexia, developmental aphasia etc. They do not include learning problems that are due primarily to visual, hearing, or motor handicaps, to mental retardation, emotional disturbance, or to environmental disadvantage.

The third step in the development of a national definition of learning disabilities came with the acceptance of a definition in relation to public Law 94-142, the Education for All Handicapped Children Act of 1975 in USA. The Bureau of Education for the Handicapped was instructed to find a better definition and to expound precisely how children can be identified as learning disabled. The Bureau made an extensive effort to develop more specific definition. Ultimately after months of lack of consensus, the following definition and criteria were published in the Federal Register (1977).

"Specific learning disability means a disorder in one or more of the basic psychological processes involved in understanding or in using language, spoken or written, which may manifest itself in an imperfect ability to listen, think, speak, read, write, spell, or to do mathematical calculation. The term includes such conditions as perceptual handicaps, brain injury, minimal brain dysfunction, dyslexia and developmental aphasia. The term does not include children who have learning problem which are primarily the result of visual, hearing, or motor handicaps, or mental retardation, of emotional disturbance, or of environmental, cultural or economic disadvantage".

CRITERIA FOR DETERMINING THE EXISTENCE OF A SPECIFIC LEARNING DISABILITY

(a) A team may determine that a child has a specific learning disability if:

(1) The child does not achieve commensurate with his or her age and ability levels in one or more of the areas listed in paragraph (a) (2) of this section, when provided with learning experiences appropriate for the child's age and ability levels; and

(2) The team finds that a child has a severe discrepancy between achievement and intellectual ability in one or more of the following areas:

i. Oral expression,
ii. Listening comprehension,
iii. Written expression,
iv. Basic reading skill,
v. Reading comprehension,
vi. Mathematics calculation, or
vii. Mathematics reasoning

b) The team may not identify a child as having a specific learning disability if the severe discrepancy between ability and achievement is primarily the result of:

i. A visual, hearing, or motor handicaps,
ii. Mental retardation
iii. Emotional disturbance, or
iv. Environmental, cultural, or economic disadvantage.

The most recent step toward development of a more acceptable definition which resolves some of the confusion was made when a revised definition was proposed by the National Joint Committee for Learning Disabilities (NJCLD) in 1981. The committee proposed the following definition that does, in the opinion of many educators, provide for more clarity and less confusion:

"Learning disabilities is a generic term that refers to a heterogeneous group of disorders manifested by significant difficulties in the acquisition and use of listening, speaking, reading, writing, reasoning and mathematical abilities. These disorders are intrinsic to the individual and presumed to be due to central nervous system dysfunction. Even though a learning

disability may occur concomitantly with other handicapping conditions (such as sensory impairment, mental retardation, social and emotional disturbance) or environmental influences (such as cultural differences, insufficient or inappropriate instruction, psychogenic factors), it is not the result of those condition or influences (P.336).

There is no end to the problem and vagueness and ambiguity with definitions of learning disabilities, at least, no solution, acceptable to a majority of advocates for the learning disabled.

From the above discussion it can be seen that learning disabilities are formally defined in many ways. However, they usually contain three essential elements. They are a discrepancy clause, an exclusion clause, and an etiology clause. The discrepancy clause asserts that there is a significant disparity between-aspects of specific functioning and general ability. The second exclusion clause states that the disparity is not due to intellectual, physical, emotional, or environmental problems. The etiology clause speaks to causation involving genetic, biochemical, or neurological factors. This last clause is often stated in definitions, but it is not focused upon since it is difficult to determine etiology and usually is not part of the educational assessment or remedial programme recommended for the students (Crealock and Kronick, 1993).

Characteristics of Students with Learning Disabilities

The main characteristics that is part of all definitions of learning disabilities is that there is a severe discrepancy between achievement and intellectual ability in some areas such as oral expression, written expression, listening comprehension, reading comprehension, reading or mathematics. Besides this basic characteristic, there are other characteristics, which are more common to students with learning disabilities than to the general population of students of their age. These characteristics are:

i. Delayed spoken language development
ii. Poor spatial orientation
iii. Inadequate time concepts
iv. Difficulty in judging relationships

v. Direction related confusion
vi. Poor general motor coordination
vii. Poor manual dexterity
viii. Social imperception
ix. Inattention
x. Hyperactivity
xi. Perceptual disorders
xii. Memory disorders.

i. Delayed Spoken Language Development

The learning disabled students lag behind in spoken language development. They will not be able to cope with their age mates or classmates. Their knowledge of vocabulary is limited. They are known for immature vocabulary also. Usually they commit large number of grammatical errors. They experience immense difficulty in relating ideas in logical sequence, and regular "groping" for words. Their language becomes disorganised when they try to discuss a number of factors simultaneously. Alternatively, they may state a proviso, but lose the main point. They most often deviate onto a tangent and forget the main point. They get confused when listening to a long or complex conversation forgetting what has been said. They simply focus on the inconsequentials rather than the important points. They find it very difficult to remember all the parts of a multisyllabic word.

ii. Poor Spatial Orientation

Learning disabled students experience unusual difficulty in becoming oriented to new surroundings. They forget their way around a complex building. They experience difficulty in assembling a complex puzzle, or executing complex mechanical tasks, and remembering how others executed multifaceted tasks. When they are faced with such a task, they may become overwhelmed and approach it randomly rather than planfully. They have difficulty in finding objects when their surroundings are busy and lack system for storing arranging, and finding their belongings.

iii. Inadequate Time Concepts

This includes regular lateness and lack of normal time concepts. There is confusion about their personal responsibility relating to time. They seldom notice how others block their time out, or what is involved in doing a task. They either overestimate the amount of time needed to complete tasks, becoming overwhelmed at what they have to do or underestimate the amount of time, leaving tasks to the last minute and becoming stressed and discouraged. Learning disabled students usually fail to observe how and why people organise, prioritise and reprioritise their time. They have a very poor sense of what time is about, that clock, calendars and date books indicate the passage of time, and that days, weeks, months, and years punctuate time. They may be unaware that units of time such as a minute, hour, or century, are fixed, or be unaware of what a century or millennium stand for, or what "19" means in "1993" (Crealock and Kronick 1993)

iv. Difficulty in Judging Relationship

Learning disabled students lack judgement concerning what is important or where importance tends to occur. As a result, they study everything, or fail to prioritise and reprioritise. These results in disorganisation, inefficiency, failure to complete the tasks and feeling overwhelmed. They experience difficulty with meanings of big Vs little, light Vs heavy, close Vs far and others. They may not notice the differences between similar sounding phonemes such as "ch"/"h", 'k'/'g' etc, which is reflected in their speech and spelling. Some of them do not understand the difference between a multiplication or addition sign, or how the various types of equations are spaced such as the indentation of numbers in multiplication, nor comprehend why such discriminations are important.

v. Direction Related Confusion

This includes difficulty in understanding of and ability to utilise concepts of right, left, north, south, east, west, up down and so on. They may not comprehend how the information of a map is translated into geographic space. They may not know which state or continent they live in, may forget which side of the road the traffic comes from and may not understand terms like north, south, east, west.

vi. Poor General Motor Coordination

This may include general clumsiness, poor coordination, poor balance, or a tendency to fall down a lot. They may be unable to do different tasks or movements with each hand simultaneously, or different movements of the hands and feet at the same time. They may be restless impatient, have a short attention span, be hyperactive or hypoactive (under active), lethargic, very disorganised. Learning disabled students may be unaware of the messages conveyed by eye contact, facial expression, movement, use of social space, gesture, dress and grooming or how others react to those aspects of themselves. They have a poor sense of the size and shape of their bodies, and what their bodies can do. Hence the poor motor coordination.

vii. Poor Manual Dexterity

This includes inability to manipulate pencils, books, or doorknobs. They also experience unusual difficulty in manipulating new equipments. In day-to-day life learning disabled students lack a sense of how to juggle their social, vocational and practical commitments. They often forget what it is they have to do, or how to execute tasks efficiently, or how to block out several tasks so that everyday aspects of their lives could be tackled with the least amount of effort and on time.

viii. Social Imperception

This includes inability to determine when other students accept him and inability to read body language (particularly facial expression) of other students and adults particularly parents and teachers. Learning disabled children have a limited repertoire of social behaviours, which bore people, rather than adjusting behaviour to context and adapting it if it is not received as expected. Further, some of the learning disabled students do not notice subtle social behaviours such as impatience or hints or the subtleties of relations such as what people do to maintain friends or express caring, or what friends and intimates contribute to relationships such as support. They are impervious to others' reactions to their behaviour, and insensitive to others needs. Research indicates that social skill deficits are common in students with learning disabilities and that these deficits have a negative effect on learning disabled students' relationship with both peers and teachers, as well as on their ability to function in the regular classroom environment.

ix. Inattention

The learning disabled students find it very difficult to focus on any one activity for the normal amount of time. Attention is the cognitive process that enables us to attend to selected features of environmental stimuli that are observed by sensory systems. For the purposes of discussion we can divide attention into two components as selective attention and sustained attention. Sustained attention refers to the degree to which attention is maintained over a period of time. Selective attention refers to ability to identify important stimuli and important aspects of a stimulus and disregard other stimuli in the environment. The learning disabled students are wanting in both. One frequent characteristics of learning disabled students is attention deficit, or inability to pay attention in class or to concentrate for long periods. This is normal in preschoolers, and among first-or second graders may simply indicate a developmental lag of little importance in the long run. However, beyond that point, attention deficits can become serious problems. Research evidences indicate that many learning disabled children do not focus on and attend selectively to the central learning task.

x. Hyperactivity

Hyper is a prefix which means "more than usual" or excessive". Activity deals with "motion" or "movement" and kinesis relates to movement and is used in medicine in relation to muscular action. Hyperactivity is a more general, non-medical word while hyperkinesis is the term that physicians use in describing children that educators would call hyperactive. Hyperactivity includes behaviour described as restless and fidgety, especially if this is an everyday, every-time-of-day phenomenon. Most of the learning disabled students are hyperactive unable to sit still, in fact, the great majority of children with attention deficits are also hyperactive. Hyperactivity is much more frequently seen in boys than in girls. Hyperactive children do tend to have many more educational problems than normal children have but it is difficult to generalise further than this.

xi. Perceptual Disorders

Perception is a person's interpretation of stimuli. Perception is the cognitive process that identifies, organises, and translates sensory data into meaningful information. Perceptual processes include discrimination, co-ordination and sequencing. Discrimination allows us to distinguish among different features within the sensory system. Coordination facilitates the integration of information from two or more information sources. Sequencing enables us to spatial and temporal stimulus sequences and patterns.

But learning disabled children may experience difficulties in any of these areas of perceptual processing. For this reason, perception has probably been the most attempted area of research in learning disabilities. The perceptual disorders include disorders of visual, auditory, tactual or kinaesthetic perception. The student with visual perceptual problem will find it very difficult to copy letters correctly or to perceive the difference of sound of the front door bell and the first ring of the telephone. The student may at first seem to be lacking in sensory acuity (that is, he may seem to have a visual loss or hearing loss) but when acuity checks out as normal it indicates that there is a prevalence of perceptual disorder.

xii. Memory Disorders

Now-a-days memory is viewed as dynamic process that enables us to take complex environmental information and to transform and organise it in a manner that permits storage and retrieval at a later time. Memory is a complex process and is not fully understood despite some researches establishing theories that seem to explain the various observable facts of memory. Memory disorders include either auditory or visual memory. Learning disabled students experience both the disorders. They may not be able to remember where the window is or on which side of the room their bed is placed, even though it has been there for months. Also, they may experience difficulty in repeating a simple sequence of three words immediately after hearing them. This sort of auditory memory deficit seriously affects the learning process. The learning disabled students are weak in short-term memory, working memory and long- term memory.

CAUSES OF LEARNING DISABILITIES

It is very difficult to specify the cause of child's learning disability. In most cases the cause of a child's learning disabilities remains a mystery. Possible causes fall into three general categories organic and biological, genetic and environmental.

ORGANIC AND BIOLOGICAL FACTORS

Many professionals believe that learning disabled children have central nervous system dysfunction. Their brains malfunction in some way. Although some authorities in this field are reluctant to favour the notion of organic or biological clauses of learning disabilities, there is an ever increasing body of research indicating that learning disabled children, especially those with severe learning difficulties, have neurological abnormalities. Early research linking organic factors and learning disabilities was based on relatively crude technological measures, but today's researchers are able to harness advanced technology to assess brain activity more precisely.

GENETIC FACTORS

There has been ever increasing evidence that indicates that learning disabilities tend to run in families. There are adequate studies implicating heredity as a cause of learning disabilities, especially severe learning disabilities, in some children. Studies of twins indicate that when one twin has a reading disability, the other is also more likely to have a reading disability, if he or she is an identical (monozygotic from the same egg) rather than a fraternal (dizygotic two eggs) twin.

ENVIRONMENTAL FACTORS

It is very difficult to document environmental causes. There is much evidence indicating that environmentally disadvantaged children are more prone to exhibit learning problems. Another possible environmental cause of learning disabilities is poor teaching. Some of authorities are of the firm opinion that if teachers were better prepared to tackle the special learning problems of children in the early school years, some learning disabilities could be avoided.

Identifying Learning Disabled Children

Procedures for Identification

Assessment is an integral part of the educational process. Educational assessment can be defined as the process of collecting data for the purpose of specifying and verifying problems and for making educational decisions about students. Data collected affect decisions regarding referral and placement, instructional planning and adaptation, and pupil progress monitoring and evaluation. There are various assessment procedures for gathering various types of information necessary for identification, and considerable additional assessment is also necessary if we are to provide an ongoing programme that will be of much value to the learning disabled student. These assessment procedures can be classified into two categories as:

i) Informal assessment
ii) Formal assessment

i) Informal assessment

Informal assessment is evaluating of information primarily gathered through observations of everyday student behaviour, through the examinations of student products such as papers, tests and presentations, and thro gh discussion with students to establish goals, select strategies, and measure outcomes. Informal assessment provides the means for systematically collecting student performance data that are instructionally relevant; it is critical to the development of effective instructional programmes. Through informal assessment procedures, teachers can directly monitor student behaviour as well as evaluate the instruction provided and the learning environment. Further, this monitoring and evaluation can be done frequently and are directly related to what is taught. There are various types of informal assessment procedures that can be used for these purposes.

TYPES OF INFORMAL ASSESSMENT

There are various types of informal assessment devices that can be used to measure characteristics of the student, the learning environment, and the success of various aspects of the instructional programme. They are:

i) Curriculum - based assessment
ii) Criterion - referenced tests
iii) Observation
iv) Interviews, questionnaires, checklists

A brief account about each of these assessment methods presented hereunder will serve as guidelines for the teachers entrusted with the task of teaching learning disabled children.

i) Curriculum - Based Assessment

Curriculum - based assessment is the process of determining instructional needs by directly assessing specific curriculum skills. The term curriculum - based assessment can be used to describe a variety of assessment techniques that measure student achievement in the curriculum. It is defined as any approach that uses direct observation and recording of a student's performance in a local school curriculum as a basis for gathering information to make instructional decisions. Gickling and associates pioneered the current movement of tieing the assessment directly to the curricula and are credited with first using the term "Curriculum - based assessment.

TYPES OF CURRICULUM - BASED ASSESSMENT

Fuchs and Deno (1991) state that most forms of curriculum - based assessment can be categorised into two major areas as specific subskill mastery measurement and general outcome measurement. In using specific subskill mastery measurement, the teachers break down a task or behaviour into specific subskills that are written as short-term objectives. Most of curriculum - based assessment systems belong to the mastery measurement model. General outcome measurement systems were developed by Deno and Colleagues to overcome the shortcomings of specific subskill mastery measurement. The most widely used types of curriculum - based assessment are:.

a) Curriculum - based measurement
b) Response and error analysis
c) Task analysis
d) Teacher made tests

a) Curriculum - Based Measurement

Curriculum - based measurement (CBM) is a form of CBA in which teachers specify long-term academic goals, conduct ongoing assessments that monitor student progress toward that goal, evaluate the adequacy of student progress and the instructional plan, and develop instructional changes that increase the probability of goal attainment. Fuchs and Deno (1991) state that CBM is a general outcome measurement that can be viewed as an effective bridge between traditional psychometric models of assessment and current observational assessment strategies in that it takes the notion of standardised measurement and applies concepts of social validity (direct observation, peer sampling, graphic display of data etc). Curriculum - based measurement has been found to positively affect student achievement and provide teachers with greater awareness of student needs and to be successful with a variety of subject matter and in a variety of settings.

b) Response and Error Analysis

Analysis of student work samples through response and error analysis is another type of CBA. Analysing student work sample supplies the teacher with valuable information for instructional planning and modification and assists in determining a student's strengths and weaknesses. The teacher can examine class assignments, projects, tests or homework assignments; or evaluate oral responses to questions or problems. Work sample analysis can be conducted in any subject. In a recent study of the use of CBM in the area of spelling, Fuchs and colleagues (1991) found that teachers who used CBM procedures effected greater gains in spelling achievement with learning disabled students than teachers who did not use CBM procedures.

In conducting a response analysis, the teacher evaluates both correct and incorrect responses by focusing on such variables as frequency, duration, rates and percentage. Response analysis data can be collected, charted, and evaluated on a daily basis and allow the teacher to examine all aspects of student performance on a task. One example of response analysis is to determine the fluency and accuracy rates of responses. Developing student's fluency at a task is essential to generalisation and application of knowledge. Increases in fluency or oral reading have been linked to increases in comprehension.

Oral reading fluency can be expressed as the number of words read correctly per minute and it can be determined by using the following equation:

$$\frac{\text{Number of words read correctly}}{\text{Total reading time in seconds}} \times 60$$

Accuracy can be defined as the number of errors committed per minute and it can be determined by using the following formula:

$$\frac{\text{Number of Effors}}{\text{Total reading time in seconds}} \times 60$$

These equations can be used to determine fluency in all subject areas. As fluency increases, the teacher should ascertain whether there is corresponding decrease in errors. Thus, the response analysis will enable the teacher to assess the learning disability of the students on the basis of their fluency and accuracy rates in the specific subject.

TABLE 6.1 SAMPLE RESPONSE ANALYSIS SHEET: MATHEMATICS

1. Activity: Addition work sheet
2. Types of items presented: 24 problems
3. Total time for students to complete the activity: 6 minute, 10 seconds
4. Number /percent of items correct: 13 items /54%
5. Number /percent of items incorrect: 11 items /46%

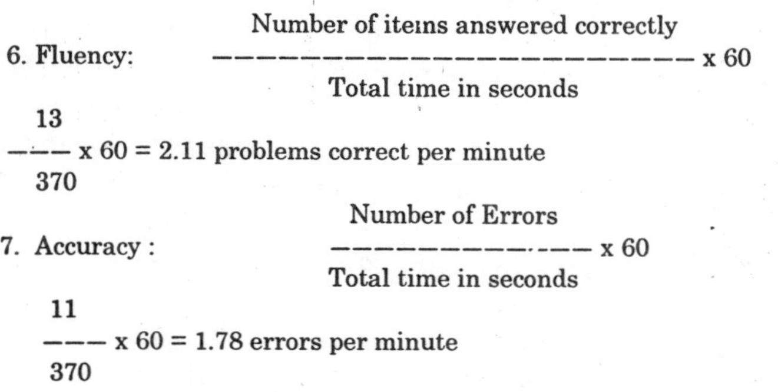

6. Fluency: $\dfrac{\text{Number of items answered correctly}}{\text{Total time in seconds}} \times 60$

$\dfrac{13}{370} \times 60 = 2.11$ problems correct per minute

7. Accuracy : $\dfrac{\text{Number of Errors}}{\text{Total time in seconds}} \times 60$

$\dfrac{11}{370} \times 60 = 1.78$ errors per minute

Error analysis is a set of procedures used to categorise a student's errors so that teaching decision can be made based on performance within the school curriculum, Errors are considered to be an important part of learning process and analysis of errors is a critical component of CBA. Although it is closely associated with response analysis, this type of analysis focuses specifically on the types of errors committed.

In error analysis, errors are classified into three categories of responses: random errors, errors in concept formation, and errors in unlearned concepts. Instruction will vary according to the errors committed by the students. If a student commits random errors, the teacher can assume that the student is capable of answering correctly but he is providing incorrect responses (possible due to carelessness). Errors in concept formation will specify the areas in which additional instruction and practice are needed to develop a basic understanding of the concept. If the students display errors due to lack of knowledge, they should receive initial instruction focused at the acquisition stage of learning. Students with learning disabilities have been found to display a substantially greater number of error responses in certain academic subjects than their nonhandicapped peers. So error analysis can be effectively made use of by the teachers to identify the learning disabled students and also to measure the degree of disability.

c) Task Analysis

Task analysis serves both as a diagnostic tool and as a basis for establishing an instructional sequence (Moyer and Dardig, 1978). It can be described as the process of identifying, breaking down, and sequencing sub - components of a target behaviour and subsequently evaluating student progress toward the attainment of those sub-component skills (Magg, 1989; Moyer and Dardig, 1978). In designing and administering task assessment, the teacher must pinpoint a target behaviour or task and write a terminal objective. The teacher then must isolate the behaviour selected and analyse it, breaking it down into teachable subtasks described in measurable terms. Once the essential sub-tasks have been determined, an assessment tool is developed containing questions at each level of the sub-task. The assessment measure is administered, and student performance data are evaluated for use in planning and implementing instruction. Based on the results of this assessment, the teacher can determine the student's entry level at a particular skill or decide where breakdowns occur in the instructional plan. This task analysis is of great value to the teacher to identify the skill or subskill in which the learning disabled students are experiencing difficulties. Task analysis will bring to light if at all there is any great disparity between different areas of functioning. This will form the basis on which the teacher can identify the learning disabled students.

d) Teacher - made Tests

Teacher - made tests are advantageous in that they are developed from the curriculum and can be used flexibly to meet a teacher's specific. Teachers know how the subject was taught and can devise an instrument that more accurately reflects student knowledge. The teacher - made tests will indicate where the students are upto mark and where they are lacking. The students may do well in some teacher - made tests pertaining to some subject and may experience difficulty in some other teacher-made tests related to certain subject or subjects. When such disparity is noticed the student is more likely to be learning disabled. Thus teacher - made tests can be effectively used to identify learning disabled students.

ii) Criterion - Referenced Tests

Criterion - referenced tests are another form of informal assessment. They are defined as assessments that rate how thoroughly students have mastered specific skills or areas of knowledge whereas norm-referenced tests are assessments that compare the performance of one student against the performance of others. Criterion-referenced tests can be either commercially developed or teacher made tests. As teacher - made tests, criterion - referenced tests are more specific to the current curriculum focus in the instructional programme. There are a number of advantages in using criterion - referenced tests over norm- referenced tests. First, the criterion - referenced tests describe the tasks that students can perform successfully. Second, criterion - referenced tests focus on limited set of tasks that are specific to the curriculum, rather than assessing a broad range of skills in an academic area. Finally, scores obtained reflect small increases in student performance that often are not detected in norm-referenced tests. Since criterion-referenced tests bring to light who is having trouble and in which area(s) he or she is having trouble, these can be effectively used by the teachers to identify the learning disabled students.

iii) Observation

Naturalistic observation is defined as the process of observing and recording behaviours in a naturalistic environment. Use of this method facilitates a broader look at behaviour as well as factors affecting behaviour. This is the most convenient and practically the foremost technique to identify learning disabled students. Observation of student's behaviour by the teacher as well as by the experts helps in identifying learning disabled students. This can be done under simple as well as controllable conditions. While making observations of the children's behaviour a strict vigil should be kept to study their reactions to various situations. A child's behaviour can be observed not only in the classroom, but also on the playground, home and in the group. Observation can be done by just scrupulously watching the child at close quarters and by moving along with the child. How he grasps the instructional presentation, how he responds in the classroom and in the school premises should be noted down and analysed properly. It should be kept in mind that the observer should have the capacity for analysing and interpreting the information he gets from his observation. Observation technique is congenial for ascertaining the curricular, co-curricular, extra-curricular and recreational interest of children. Also, it enables the teacher to notice manifestations of certain lack and disorders, which are unique characteristics of learning disabled children.

II. Formal Assessment

In addition to the mandate that a learning disability can not be identified by a single assessment instrument or person (USOE, 1977), the basic diagnostic process is the same regardless of the disability. The diagnosis of any disability is not an event. It is rather a goal-oriented process that is guided by a series of questions posed at each stage. To answer the questions, members of the multidisciplinary team obtain data from a variety of procedures and tests. At several stages in the process, the same tests might be used for students who may be retarded, emotionally disturbed, learning disabled or normal. It is not the use of a special test, but the results obtained at each stage in the process that lead to the identification of a learning disability, a different disability or no disability.

Formal assessment usually employs individually administered tests that have been standardised, in that they consist of a set of tasks given with uniform directions and compare performance to an identified standard. The tests that are known as norm-referenced compare scores with the average performance (norm) for a clearly defined and representative group of individuals. Typically, norm - referenced instruments are used for identification purposes because they (1) provide information about the referred individual relative to peers, and (2) have the mathematical adequacy to be used in complex calculations that

TABLE 6.2. STANDARDIZED INSTRUMENTS: INTELLIGENCE DOMAIN

Test	Ages	Score	Domains/Subtests
Wechsler Intelligence Scale for Children-Revised (WISC-R) (1974)	6-0 to 16-6	Full Scale IQ	Verbal IQ; Performance IQ
Wechsler Preschool and Primary Scale of Intelligence-Revised (WPPSI-R) (1989)	3-0 to 7-3	Full Scale IQ	Verbal IQ; Performance I Q
Wechsler Adult Intelligence Scale-Revised (WAIS-R) (1981)	16 to 74	Full Scale IQ	Verbal IQ; Performance IQ
Stanford-Binet Intelligence Scale; fourth Edition (SB:FE) (1986)	2-6 to 23-11	Composite, Standard Age Score (SAS)	Verbal Reasoning, Abstract/ Visual Reasoning, Quantitative Reasoning, Short-term Memory
Kaufman Assessment Battery for Children (K-ABC) (1983)	2-6 to 12-5	Mental Processing, Compositescore	Sequential Processing Scale, Simultaneous Processing Scale
Woodcock - Johnson Psycho educational Battery, Revised (WJ-R) (1977)	3-09 to 80+	Broad Cognitive Ability score	Reading, Mathematics, Written language, and Knowledge Aptitude
Woodcock-Johnson Psycho educational Battery,			

{Cont}....

Revised (WJ-R) (1989) Reading, mathematics, Written language,	2-0 to 90+	Broad Cognitive Ability score	Oral language, Knowledge Aptitude; 8 additional processing scales
Detroit Tests of Learning Aptitude (DTLA-2) 91985)	6 through 18	General Linguistic, Quotient	Intelligence Cognitive, Attentional, and Motor domains
Differential Ability Scales (DAS)	2-6 to 17	Cognitive Ability score	Speed of information processing; verbal, nonviable, quantitative reasoning; spatial imagery; perceptual matching; memory
Hiskey-Nebraska Test of Learning Aptitude (BNTLA)(1966)	3 to 16	Deviation Learning Quotient	12 subtests of verbal labeling, categorization, concept formation, and rehearsal (no verbal direction or responses required)

are part of the identification and eligibility criteria. There are quite a number of tests employed in formal assessment for identification of learning disability and a detailed description of these tests has been presented by Reddy, Ramar, and Kusuma (1999) in their text 'Learning Disabilities: A Practical Guide to Practitioners.

EDUCATIONAL PROGRAMMES FOR LEARNING DISABLED CHILDREN

There are several possible orientations for planning intervention programmes for learning disabled children. The following categories reflect what the majority of the professionals recognise as the major approaches.

1. Behavioural Interventions
2. Cognitive behavioural interventions
3. Medically based interventions
4. Multisensory approach
5. Direct instruction

In practice, a teacher can combine two or more of these approaches. A judicious blend of the above approaches is bound to yield fruitful results.

i) Behavioural Interventions

Applied behavioural analysis focuses on changing socially significant behaviours that have been observed and operationally defined. Environmental factors can be systematically manipulated to increase, decrease, change or shape targeted responses. Behavioural interventions should generally be attempted first because they are easy to initiate in the context of the classroom and do not require the intervention of other professionals or experts. In designing behavioural interventions the teacher teaching learning disabled students should first prioritise individual needs and then select target behaviour. The teacher should select out-of-seat behaviour as the first behaviour to be targeted because it forms the base for distraction or inattention. Out-of-seat behaviour refers to the behaviour of the learning disabled students when he was not in contact with the task. Reinforcement of incompatible behaviour should be used to reduce the frequency of out-of-seat behaviour. The learning disabled students must be reinforced for remaining in their seats. The teacher may provide reinforcement such as token economy as well as praise for staying in their seats. If the teacher increases the amount of time the learning disabled children spend in their seat, their on-desk behaviour and productivity will proportionately increase.

Research supports the effectiveness of behavioural interventions for a variety of behaviours including attention problems. Contingency contracting, peer-mediated interventions, token economies, time-out- from positive reinforcement and other reductive procedures based on reinforcement have been successfully utilised to deal with problems with attention. Hence, the teachers should utilise a behavioural intervention as the initial option of choice in the elimination of the problem, when they observe attention problems among learning disabled students. Since specific behavioural interventions have already been discussed in detail in this chapter, they are not elaborated here to avoid redundancy.

ii) Cognitive Behavioural Interventions

Cognitive behavioural instruction has been used for téaching students to act as their own behaviour change agents. Self-monitoring is the most appropriate strategy for intervention of attention behaviours. Self-monitoring is the ability to repeatedly evaluate one's own behaviours in order to effect positive change in those. Self-monitoring has been successfully used among population with disabilities, including those with learning disabilities. Research supports the effectiveness of self-monitoring for increasing on-task behaviours.

Broden and colleagues (1971), in their classic study of self-monitoring, analysed the effects of self-recording on the behaviour of two eighth grade students using an ABABCDA design. In the experiment, during the first phase the subjects were observed by trained observers for 30 minutes per day throughout the study. It was found that the students under study evinced appropriate attentional behaviours (e.g., facing the teacher, taking notes when appropriate) only 30% of the time.

Then they were given self-monitoring treatment in which they were given a recording sheet with the printed direction to record their attending behaviours whenever they thought of it by marking a + when they were on task and a - when they were not. During the next phase, self-recording was continued with the addition of the condition of praise by the teacher for good study habits. After that, self-recording was withdrawn and the praise was continued. The study was concluded with a return to initial phase. The obtained results established that their attention behaviours improved during treatment phases. Also, the frequency of these behaviours remained at relatively high levels when self-monitoring and praise were withdrawn.

iii) Medically Based Interventions

Medical science can play a major role if the attention problems are due to hyperactivity. If a student is hyperactive, he or she is more likely to have difficulty with learning. When there are attention problems, educational remedies such as behavioural interventions and self-monitoring interventions should be applied. If these intervention strategies do not alleviate the problem, a drug intervention may be attempted.

TYPE OF DRUG INTERVENTIONS

Often the medication chosen for hyperactivity and attention problems is one in the amphetamine family. The three stimulant medications most often prescribed for attention deficit disorder are Cylert, Ritalin, and Dexedrine. These medications vary in terms of their effectiveness and duration of action. Ritalin and Dexedrine become effective in less than half an hour but Cylert takes upto four weeks. There is a striking contrast in the duration of action also. Cylert is taken once a day and its effects are long-lasting whereas the effect of Ritalin and Dexedrine last for three to five hours only. Therefore, it becomes necessary for a second dose to be administered at school. It poses administrative problems.

There is some concern about side effects of medication as well as possible abuse. An ideal medication controls hyperactivity, increases attention, and reduces impulsive and suggestive behaviours without inducing anorexia, drowsiness, insomnia, headaches, or other side effects. Side effects are usually relatively minor and temporary and tend to diminish as tolerance develops, although effects vary from individual to individual.

EFFECTIVENESS OF DRUG INTERVENTION

Numerous studies have shown that medically based interventions are effective in controlling problem behaviours in the classroom. Some research indicates that drug intervention improves academic classwork as well as behaviour. However, parents and teachers are often more interested in performance on standardised achievement tasks, where the impact of drug interventions has been only modest. Further research is needed in which longitudinal studies are used to track children for a number of years to determine whether they think, learn, and socially function more effectively with medication, not whether they are quicker, more attentive, or productive in one particular situation.

MULTISENSORY APPROACH

A number of programmes have been developed for training visual and visual motor skills as well as psycholinguistic processes. Multisensory programmes very much emphasise working with academic materials directly. Multisensory methods use a combination of the child's sensory systems in the training process. The underlying assumption is that if more than one sense is involved in learning experiences, the children will learn better.

The prototype of most Multisensory approaches is Fernald's VAKT method. (V stands for Visual, A for auditory, K for kinesthetic and T for tactual). In the first step, the child tells the teacher a story. The teacher notes down the words of the story, which serves as the materials as the child learns to read. Using children's own story is a particularly good motivator, especially for older children. In learning the words, the child first sees the word (visual) then hears the teacher say the word (auditory). Next the child says the word (auditory), and finally, the child traces the word (kinaesthetic and tactual).

DIRECT INSTRUCTION

Direct instruction is a complex way of looking at all aspects of instruction, including classroom organisation and management, the quality of teacher-student interaction, the design of instructional materials, and the nature of inservice teacher training. Learning disabled students who are taught using direct instruction significantly outperform other learning disabled students instructed through indirect methods. Rosenshine (1979) has summarised the principal prescriptions of direct instruction as follows:

Direct instruction refers to academically focused, teacher directed classrooms using sequenced and structured materials. It refers to teaching activities where goals are clear to students, time allocated for instruction is sufficient and continuous, coverage of content is extensive, the performance of students is monitored....and feed back to students is immediate and academically oriented. In direct instruction the teacher controls the instructional goals, chooses materials appropriate for the student's ability, and paces the instructional episode. Interaction is..... structured, but not authoritarian Learning takes place in a convivial academic atmosphere (Rosenshine, 1979).

Simply speaking direct instruction is an approach to teaching in which lessons are goal oriented and structured by the teacher. Direct instruction differs from other behavioural education approaches in its degree of emphasis on the antecedent stimuli. In direct instruction, specific antecedent stimuli that are emphasised include the precise nature of teacher wording examples, and how teachers present new material to students. The control of environmental variables in a teaching situation is dependent upon faultless communication. Instructional materials and teachers' delivery must be clear and unambiguous for faultless communication to take place. Therefore, many direct instruction materials provide "scripts" to teachers to use during the instructional process.

SUMMARY

The field of learning disabilities is the newest challenging sub-area of the broader field of special education. It is learning disabilities that are the most vague and mystifying when compared to other major handicapping or disabling conditions. Kirk used the term learning disabilities to describe children who had disorders in development in language, speech, reading and associated communication skills needed for social interaction.

Characteristics of learning disabled children include delayed spoken language development, poor spatial orientation, inadequate time concepts, difficulty in judging relationships, direction related confusion, poor general motor coordination, poor manual dexterity, social imperception, inattention ,hyperactivity, perceptual disorders and memory disorders. Organic and biological factors, genetic factors and environmental factors are the possible causes of learning disabilities.

Learning disabled children can be identified by using both formal and informal measures. Informal assessment includes curriculum - based assessment, criterion-referenced tests, observation and interviews, questionnaires and checklists. Formal assessment includes standardised tests which can be grouped under three categories as measures of intelligence, measures of academic functioning, and measures of certain cognitive areas.

Educational programmes for learning disabled children include behavioural intervention, cognitive behavioural intervention, medically based interventions, multisensory approach and direct instruction.

REFERENCES

Crealock, C., and Kronick, D. (1993) *Children and Young people with Specific Learning Disabilities*. In Guides for Special Educations No. 9, UNESCO, Paris.

Gearheart, B.R. (1985) *Learning Disabilities: Educational Strategies.* Times Mirror /Mosby, Toronto.

Hallahen, D.P., and Karffman, J.M. (1991) *Exceptional Children.* Prentice - Hall, Englewood Cliffs, N.J.

Reddy, G.L., Ramar, R., and Kusuma, A. (1999) *Learning Disabilities: A Practical Guide to Practitioners.* Discovery Publishing House, New Delhi.

Smith, D.H. (1986) *Teaching the Learning Disabled.* Prentice-Hall, Englewood Cliffs, N.J

7

STUDENTS WITH EMOTIONAL\BEHAVIOURAL DISORDERS

OBJECTIVES

This chapter deals with students with emotional/behavioural disorders. Their characteristics and causes of their disorders are also described. The educational programmes for these students are discussed. After reading the chapter, the readers should be able to:

1. Understand the concept and causes of emotional/behavioural disorders.
2. Enumerate the characteristics of students with emotional/behavioural disorders.
3. Identify students with emotional/behavioural disorders.
4. Design intervention as well as educational programmes for students with emotional behavioural disorders.

Children with emotional/behavioural disorders are not generally good at making friends. Their serious problem is their failure to establish close and satisfying emotional ties with other people. Other children are not attracted to them and adults do no find them pleasant to be around. The only friends they may be able to find are imaginary ones.

All students are likely to have emotional problems at some point in their school career, but about one percent have such serious, long lasting and pervasive emotional disorders that they require special education. As in the case of learning disabilities, students with serious emotional disorders are more likely to be boy than girls, by a ratio of more than three to one. Many children with emotional /behavioural disorders are isolated from others not because they withdraw from friendly advances but because they strike out with hostility and aggression. These students are more likely to be abusive, destructive, unpredictable, irresponsible, bossy, quarrelsome, irritable, jealous, deficient anything but pleasant to be with. Hence, it is natural that other children and adults do not like to spend time with these children unless they have to. Most of them tend to strike back at children with these disorders. It is therefore no wonder that these children seem to be embroiled in a continuous battle with everyone.

DEFINITIONS

Many different terms have been used to designate children who have extreme social-interpersonal and/or intrapersonal problems, including emotionally handicapped, emotionally impaired, behaviourally impaired, socially /emotionally handicapped, emotionally conflicted, having personal and social adjustment problems, and seriously behaviourally disabled. These terms do not designate distinctly different types of disorders. As such there is no universally accepted definition of students with emotional /behavioural disorders. Professional groups and experts construct individual working definitions to suit their own professional purposes.

There are various reasons for the lack of consensus regarding definition. Defining emotional /behavioural disorder is somewhat like defining familiar experience: anger, loneliness, or happiness, for example. But providing an objective definition is far from simple. The factors that make it particularly difficult to arrive at a good definition of emotional /behavioural disorder are as follows.

Lack of an adequate definition of mental health and normal behaviour.

- Differences among conceptual models.
- Difficulties in measuring emotions and behaviour.
- Relationships between emotional/behavioural disorders and other handicapping conditions.
- Differences in the functions of socialisation agents who categorise and serve children.

However, although the terminology used and the relative emphasis given to certain points vary considerably from one definition to another, seriously emotionally disturbed children can be defined as those whose educational performance is adversely affected over a long period of time to a marked degree by any of the following conditions.

1. An inability to learn which can not be explained by intellectual, sensory, or health factors.
2. An inability to build or maintain satisfactory interpersonal relationships with peers and tutors.
3. Inappropriate types of behaviour or feelings under normal circumstances.
4. A general, pervasive mood of unhappiness or depression.
5. A tendency to develop physical symptoms, pains or fears associated with personal or school problems.

Children who are schizophrenic or autistic, fall under this category, but the children who are socially maladjusted, unless it is determined that they are seriously emotionally disturbed, do not fall under the category of children with emotional/ behavioural disorders.

CLASSIFICATION OF EMOTIONAL/BEHAVIOURAL DISORDERS.

There are many ways to have emotional /behavioural disorder. Hence it is reasonable to expect that students can be grouped into subcategories according to the types of problems they have. Still there is no generally acceptable, system for classifying emotional /behavioural disorder for special education.

Achenbach and others have classified two broad, pervasive dimensions of disordered behaviour: externalising and internalising. Externalising behaviour includes striking out against others while internalising behaviour involves mental or emotional conflicts such as depression and anxiety. There are a variety of more specific dimensions found by several researchers. For example, Quay and Peterson (1987) describe six dimensions characterised by the following kinds of behaviour.

1. Conduct Disorder
    - E/BD children try to seek attention.
    - They are marked for show off behaviour.
    - They are disruptive and annoys others.
    - They evince temper tantrums and fight frequently.
2. Socialised Aggression
    - They steal in company with others.
    - They remain loyal to delinquent friends.
    - They are truant from school with others.
    - They have "bad" companions.
    - They freely admit disrespect for moral values and laws.
3. Attention Problems and Immaturity
    - They are known for short attention span.
    - Their power of concentration is markedly poor.
    - They are easily distractible and diverted from the task at hand.
    - They are sluggish, slow moving and lethargic.
    - They tend to answer without thinking.
4. Anxiety - withdrawal
    - They are self-conscious
    - They are easily embarrassed
    - They are usually hypersensitive
    - Their feelings are easily hurt.
    - They are generally fearful and anxious.
    - They are depressed and always sad.
5. Psychotic Behaviour
    - Emotionally /behaviourally disordered children express far fetched ideas.

- They are marked for repetitive speech
- They evince bizarre behaviour.

Motor Excess

- They are restless and unable to sit still.
- They are tense and unable to relax.
- They are overtalkative.

CHARACTERISTICS OF STUDENTS WITH EMOTIONAL /BEHAVIOURAL DISORDERS

There are scores of characteristics associated with the area of emotional disturbance. The important issue is the degree of the behaviour problem. Actually any behaviour exhibited excessively over a long period of time might be considered an indication of emotional disturbance. There are some general characteristics manifested by most students identified as emotionally disturbed. These include poor academic achievement, poor interpersonal relationship, poor self-esteem, aggressive behaviour withdrawn and immature behaviour and hyperactivity. A brief discussion of each of the characteristics is furnished below.

POOR ACADEMIC ACHIEVEMENT

Research evidences indicate that the average child with emotional/behavioural disorder has an IQ in the dull normal range (around 90) and that relatively few score above the bright normal range. More children with emotional /behavioural disorder fall into the slow learner and mildly retarded categories. IQ is relatively a good predictor of how far a child will progress academically and socially, even in cases of severe and profound disorders. Most children with emotional /behavioural disorders are also under-achievers at school. A child with emotional / behavioural disorder is not able to achieve at the level expected for his or her mental age. It is rarity to find these students academically advanced.

POOR INTERPERSONAL RELATIONSHIPS

Students with emotional /behavioural disorders are not well liked by their peers. Studies of the social status of students in regular elementary and secondary classrooms have indicated that the students identified as having emotional /behavioural disorders are seldom socially accepted. They are not able to maintain a good interpersonal relationship with others. Research studies show that children whether normal or exceptional who are in frequent conflict with authority, who fight or bother others a great deal, and who demonstrate verbal aggression are rarely the objects of social acceptance. Since the children with emotional /behavioural disorder evince these characteristics, they are actively rejected, not just neglected, by their peers.

AGGRESSIVE BEHAVIOUR

Most of the emotionally disturbed children engage in aggressive "acting out" behaviour from time to time. They are more likely to engage in fighting, stealing, destruction of property, refusal to obey teachers, and other behaviours that are unacceptable in schools. They do not respond to punishment or threats, though they may be quite devious and skilled at avoiding punishment. Aggressive children pose a threat to the school and to their peers and also they can put themselves in grave danger. Aggressive children, particularly boys, are likely to develop serious emotional problems later in life. They are likely to have difficulty in holding jobs and to become involved in criminal behaviour.

WITHDRAWN AND IMMATURE BEHAVIOUR

While the aggressive children cause distressing problems to teachers and peers, children who are withdrawn, immature, low in self-esteem, or depressed can be just as disturbed. Such students have few or no friends at all. They may play with children much younger than themselves. They have elaborate fantasies or daydreams and have either very low self-images or grandiose visions of themselves. They tend to be overly anxious about their health and feel generally ill at stressful situations. Some of the emotionally disturbed children evince school phobia refusing to attend school or running away from school. Unlike aggressive children, who look normal when they are not aggressive, withdrawn and immature children often appear odd or awkward and at all times.

An important aspect of withdrawn, immature behavioural is depression. Depression can also be caused by environmental or psychological factors such as the death of a loved one, separation of ones parents, school failure, rejection by peers, or a chaotic and punitive home environment. Withdrawn and immature students almost always suffer from a lack of social skills. Successful therapies for these children involve teaching them the social skills that other students absorb without special instruction. Research studies have established that social skills training programmes have been quite effective in improving the social behaviour of withdrawn friendless students, and in increasing their acceptance by their classmates.

HYPERACTIVITY

Another characteristic of students with emotional and behavioural disorders is hyperactivity. These students are unable to sit still or to concentrate for any length of time. Hyperactive children exhibit excessive restlessness and short attention span. Hyperactive students are often described as "always on the go" as though "driven by a motor". Students diagnosed as hyperactive are often given stimulant medication, such as Ritalin or Dexedrine. These drugs usually do make them more manageable and sometimes, improve their academic performance. At the same time, nondrug therapies such as the behaviour management methods can be as effective as or more effective than medication.

CAUSES OF EMOTIONAL /BEHAVIOURAL DISORDERS

The causes of emotional /behavioural disorders can be attributed to four major factors: biological disorders and diseases, pathological family relationship, negative cultural influences, and undesirable experiences at school. It is not easily possible to assert with conclusive empirical evidence that any of these factors is directly responsible for emotional /behavioural disorder. However, it is apparent that some may give child a predisposition to manifest problem behaviour, and others may precipitate or trigger it. Another concept is the idea of contributing factors. It is extremely unusual to find a single cause that has led directly to the disordered behaviour. Usually several factors join together to contribute to the development of a problem. A brief discussion of each of the causative factors is presented hereunder.

BIOLOGICAL FACTORS

Behaviour is likely to be influenced by genetic, neurological, or biochemical factors, or by combinations of these. There is no denying that there is a relationship between body and behaviour. Hence it is quite reasonable to look for a biological causal factor for certain emotional /behavioural disorders. All children are born with a biologically determined behavioural style, or temperament. Children with difficult temperaments are predisposed to develop emotional /behavioural disorder. There are other biological factors such as disease, malnutrition, and brain trauma that may predispose children to develop emotional problems. Psychotic (autistic or schizophrenic. Also it is now generally accepted that autism is a neurological disorder, but the nature and causes of the neurological defect are not known.

FAMILY FACTORS

Mental health specialists blame behavioural difficulties primarily on parent child relationship. It is because nuclear family-father, mother, and children- has a profound influence on early development. Some advocates of psychoanalysis are of the opinion that almost all severe problems of children stern from early negative interactions between the mother and child. Family influences are interactional and transactional and the effects of parents and children on one another are reciprocal. The outcome of parental discipline depends not only on the particular techniques used but also on the characteristics of the child. Sensitivity to children's needs, love oriented methods of dealing with misbehaviour, and reinforcement for appropriate behaviour by way of attention or praise tend to promote desirable behaviour in children. Parents who are generally lax in disciplining their children but are hostile rejecting, cruel, and inconsistent in dealing with misbehaviour are more likely to have aggressive and delinquent children. Similarly children from broken, disorganised homes in which the parents themselves have arrest records or are violent, are particularly likely to develop emotional /behavioural disorders.

CULTURAL FACTORS

It is a known fact that children and parents are embedded in a culture that influences their behaviour. Many environmental conditions affect adults' expectations of children and children's expectations for themselves and their peers. It is the culture that communicates values and behavioural standards to children. Undoubtedly, the culture in which the children are reared exerts an influence on their emotional, social, and behavioural development. Case studies of rapidly changing cultures bear this out. Cultural conditions, demands, prohibitions and models such as the use of terror as means of coercion, the availability of recreational drugs and the level of drug use, changing standards for several conduct, religious demands and restrictions on behaviour influences the emotions /behaviours of children to a considerable extent. The level of violence depicted on television and in movies is a contributing factor to the increasing level of violence in our society. It is much distressing to note that television violence seems more "real" to disturbed than to non-disturbed children. Research findings indicate that disturbed children may be more likely than others to perform aggressive acts after watching violence depicted on TV and in movies.

SCHOOL FACTORS

Some children come to school already with emotional and behavioural disorders; others develop emotional or behavioural disorders during their school years, perhaps in part because of damaging experiences in the classroom itself. Children who come to school with emotional /behavioural disorder, may become better or worse according to how they are managed in the class room. A child's temperament and social competence may interact with classmates' and teachers' behaviour in contributing to emotional /behavioural problems. A child entering school with already difficult temperament is likely to get negative responses from peers and teachers. Such children become trapped in a spiral of negative interactions in which they become increasingly irritating to and irritated by peers and teachers. The school can positively contribute to the development of emotional problems in several rather specific ways. Teachers may be insensitive to children's individuality and they may require a mindless conformity to the rules and routines. Educators as well as parents may hold too high or too low expectations for the child's achievement or conduct. Discipline in the school may be too lax, too rigid, or inconsistent. Instructions may be inappropriate. The school environment may be such that the misbehaving child is rewarded with recognition and special attention, even if that attention is criticism or punishment. Finally, teachers and peers may be models of misconduct and so the child may misbehave imitating them.

IDENTIFYING CHILDREN WITH EMOTIONAL /BEHAVIOURAL DISORDERS

It is easier to identify disordered behaviours than it is to define and classify types and causes of emotional /behavioural disorder. Most of the children with emotional/behavioural disorder do not elude the notice of the teachers. Occasionally one or two may remain invisible without being a bother to anyone, but it is usually easy for experienced teachers to identify children with emotional /behavioural disorders. The most common type of emotional /behavioural disorder-conduct disorder-attracts immediate attention of the teacher and there is no problem in identification.

PROBLEM IN IDENTIFICATION

It is very difficult to judge whether or not the child's behaviour signifies a serious problem when the child is young. Sometimes the children with emotional /behavioural disorders remain undetected since the teachers are not sensitive to their problems. At times, these children do not stand out sharply from other children in the environment who may have even more serious problems. Moreover, even sensitive teachers sometimes make errors of judgement. Finally, some children with emotional / behavioural disorder do not exhibit problems at school.

INFORMAL PROCEDURE

Formal screening and accurate early identification for the purpose of planning educational intervention are complicated by the problems of definition of emotional /behavioural disorder. Teacher's informal judgement has served as a fairly valid and reliable means of screening children for emotional /behavioural problems. The teacher can effectively make use of observation techniques to identify children with emotional /behavioural problems in his classroom.

OBSERVATION

Classroom observation indicates the extent to which the child meets academic expectations; playground observations are useful to assess the quality and nature of social behaviour. These direct observations of behaviour will aid the teacher to decide whether or not the child has problems that warrant classification for special education. Once the children are identified on the basis of observation, they can be subjected to more formal screening for confirmation.

FORMAL PROCEDURE

Formal assessment is a must to complement identification. Formal screening systems may lead to improved services for children with emotional /behavioural disorder. Children with emotional /behavioural disorders are so easily identified by the school personnel, that few schools bother to use systematic screening procedures. However, an insight into the formal screening procedures will provide the teachers with better preparedness to tackle emotional /behavioural disorder.

THREE STEP PROCESS

Walker and his colleagues have devised a screening system for use in elementary schools. Teachers tend to overrefer students who manifest externalising behaviour problems and underrefer students with internalising problems. To make certain that children are not overlooked in screening, but that a lot of time and effort is not wasted, a three step process is used.

Step 1 - The teacher lists and rank-orders students with externalising and internalising problems. The children who best fit descriptions of students with externalising problems and the children who best fit the descriptions of students with internalising problems are listed. Than the listed children are rankordered from most like to least like descriptions.

Step 2 - The teacher completes two checklists for the three highest ranked children on each list. One checklist asks the teacher to indicate whether each pupil manifested specific behaviours during the past month such as 'steals', "has tantrums", "uses obscene language or wears". The other checklists requires the teacher to judge how often each child shows certain characteristics (e.g. "follows established classroom rules" or "co-operates with peers in group activities or situations").

Step 3 - Children whose scores on these checklists exceed established norms are observed in the classroom and on the playground by a school professional other than the classroom teacher. He may be a school psychologist, counsellor or a resource teacher.

As in any identification system, here too both formal assessment measures and informal assessment measures complement each other. Once the children are identified as students with emotional /behavioural disorders, they should be treated with special educational programmes so that they can be enabled to surmount their problem.

Educational Programmes for Children with Emotional /Behavioural Disorder

t is rare to come across coherent, comprehensive descriptions of educational programmes for students with emotional / behavioural disorders. Even the few programmes now available also lack adequate details about such critical elements as guiding philosophy, goals, definition of the students to be served, criteria for entry into and exit from the programme, and educational methods. Also, the special educators and mental health professionals differ on their views regarding how to educate children with emotional /behavioural disorders. There are many different views regarding the education of children with emotional /behavioural disorders. Brief sketches of several different approaches to teach children with emotional / behavioural disorder are provided hereunder.

THE PSYCHOANALYTIC APPROACH

Psychiatrists and clinical psychologists primarily formulated this particular approach to education. They believe that the guiding principles of psychoanalysis can be used in education. They view the problems of emotional /behavioural disorder as pathological imbalance among the dynamic parts of the mind: id, ego, and superego. Educational practices are designed to help uncover the underlying mental pathology in an effort to improve psychological functioning, as well as behaviour and achievement.

Important features of this approach are:

- This approach lays emphasis on building a teacher - pupil relationship in which the children feel accepted and free to act out their impulses in a permissive environment.
- The major concern of the teacher is to enable the children to surmount underlying mental conflicts, not to change the surface behaviour or to teach academic skills.
- The children and parents receive therapy and the psychotherapists help the children "work through" problems in theory session.

The Psychoeducational Approach

Those who developed psycho educational approach have attempted to interweave psychiatric and educational concerns. Problems of children with emotional /behavioural disorder involve both underlying psychiatric disorders and observable misbehaviour and underachievement. So there is a balance between therpurtic goals and goals for achievement in the educational practices. This approach stresses the following educational practices.

- Unconscious motivation and underlying pathology must be taken into account.
- There must be also concern for the management of surface behaviour and academic achievement.
- This approach lays emphasis on meeting the individual needs of children.
- Teaching must involve projects or the creative arts such as music, art and dance.

THE HUMANISTIC APPROACH

The humanistic approach to education of children with emotional /behavioural disorders evolved out of humanistic psychology. According to humanistic educators the basic problem of children with emotional /behavioural disorders is that they are out of touch with their own feelings and can not find meaning and self-fulfilment in traditional classroom settings. So this approach recommends the following educational practices.

- Children's self-direction, self-evaluation, and emotional involvement in learning in non-traditional settings must be enhanced
- The teacher must function as a resource and catalyst for children's learning rather than as a director of activities.
- Children and teachers must work together as learners, pursuing areas of interest to themselves and sharing information.
- Non-authoritarian, self-directed, self-evaluative, affective, open and personal are words used to describe humanistic education for disturbed children.

THE ECOLOGICAL APPROACH

Proponents of the ecological approach are of the opinion that children with emotional /behavioural disorder experience problems in interaction with various elements of environment such as school, family, community and social agencies. The child is viewed as a disturber of the environment, and his or her behaviour is viewed as disturbing as it is disturbed. These theorists borrow the concepts from biological ecology and ecological psychology. They suggest that educational practices must be part of a strategy to alter the entire social system in which the child is unmasked. This approach emphasises the following.

- Mere intervention in the child's behaviours will not suffice. The environment must be changed enough to support desirable behaviour once the intervention is over.
- There must be concern not only for the effective teaching of the children but also for work with the children's family, neighbourhood, and community agencies.
- The teacher should teach specific and useful skills including academics, recreation and everyday living skills.

THE BEHAVIOURAL APPROACH

This approach to education of children with emotional / behavioural disorders is based on the principles of operant and respondent conditioning. Behavioural problems represent inappropriate learning. Children can be helped when their observable behaviours is modified. Modification of behaviour can be effectuated by manipulation of the child's behaviour. The main focus of concern in this approach is the child's behaviour. This approach recommends the following educational practices.

- The children's behaviours must be precisely measured.
- Educational practices must be clearly specified and analysed for their effects on the behaviours being measured.
- Observable problem behaviours must be measured and the consequences of the behaviour must be manipulated in order to change them.

TEACHING STUDENTS WITH EMOTIONAL/BEHAVIOURAL DISORDERS IN GENERAL EDUCATION CLASSROOM

Recognising students with emotional /behavioural disorders is sometimes easy and sometimes complex. Some children with emotional/behavioural disorders are aggressive. It is relatively easy to identify them because they act out in ways that are obviously inappropriate for school. On the otherhand, some students with emotional/behavioural disorder are withdrawn. It is relatively difficult to identify them because they exhibit more subtle behaviours. In the context of a busy classroom, it is not easy to identify them. The teacher should identify the students with emotional/behavioural disorders and design appropriate instructional strategy to enhance their learning.

TEACHING TECHNIQUES TO TRY

There are several approaches to the treatment of children with emotional/behavioural disorders. But the following technique is often used by the teachers. It involves identifying the factors in school that contribute to the students' inappropriate behaviour, and the factors in school that can be altered to change those behaviours. Intervention programme must include helping students to increase appropriate behaviour, decrease inappropriate over, and learn behaviours they do not know already.

To manage students' behaviour Lewis and Doorlag (1987) suggest that teachers follow a step-by-step process.

1. Stating the behavioural expectations for all the students in the classroom.
2. Determining whether students who meet these expectations are receiving reinforcement so they will continue to meet the expectations.
3. If there are students, who do not meet the expectations, determining whether they understand the expectations and whether they have the needed skills to perform the behaviours.
4. For students who use inappropriate behaviours identifying a behaviour to change.
5. Deciding how to observe and gather information on the particular behaviour.
6. Determining whether the behaviour needs to be increased, decreased, or learned, after reviewing the information collected.
7. Choosing a strategy that is positive rather than punishing.

8. Collecting information on the student's behaviour while using the strategy.
9. Reviewing this information to decide whether this strategy should be continued modified or stopped.
10. When the student performs the behaviour at the desired level, continuing to monitor and returning to step 4 if the student has other behaviours that require intervention.

INCREASING APPROPRIATE SCHOOL BEHAVIOUR

The best way to increase a student's appropriate behaviour is to reward that behaviour when the student exhibits it. The reward can take many forms. The teacher may give a point or token exchangeable at a later time for a special privilege. The reward may be in the form of a positive comment, such as "good work", "I liked the way you worked yourself on the math problems". However, it is not that all students like the same rewards. So the teacher must find the one that works with a particular student or groups of students. Rewards such as being a team leader, having extra computer time, and eating lunch with a friend can also work with some students.

In this approach, it is the timing of the reward that matters most. It is important to provide the teachers with rewards as soon as the teacher observes them demonstrating appropriate behaviour. Delaying the reward will not be much effective. Once the student manifests appropriate behaviour regularly, the teacher should gradually decrease the frequency of the reward until the student continues to use the behaviour at the specified level with less frequent rewards.

DECREASING INAPPROPRIATE SCHOOL BEHAVIOURS

As there are some students who need help in increasing appropriate behaviour so are there some students who need help in decreasing inappropriate behaviour. There are several techniques to decrease inappropriate behaviour but many of them involve some types of punishment to be carefully administered by trained professionals. Punishment can be defined as any consequence that results in reduction in the frequency or strength of a specific behaviour. So the teachers can resort to mild punishment strategies such as mild reprimands, purposeful ignoring of a student's behaviour, and withholding other rewards. These strategies combined with positive rewards when student exhibits appropriate behaviour will be very effective. Punishments and rewards must be managed carefully and used consistently as suggested in the ten-step process already discussed. Another strategy that the teachers can use is to reinforce a desirable behaviour that is incompatible with the one they want to decrease.

BEHAVIOURAL CONTRACT

Teachers can use still another technique called a behavioural contract. It systematises the use of reinforcement. This written agreement between adults and students is often called a contingency contract as it specifics what rewards and consequences will result from, the student's performance of a specific behaviour. Like any contract its contents are negotiated and all participants must agree to its terms. A contract states the

- Behaviour to be performed
- Condition under which the behaviour will be performed
- Criterion for successful performance of the behaviour.
- Reward for performing the behaviour
- Consequences for failing to perform the behaviour.
- Signatures of the participants.
- Date (Teachers who plan to use several contracts to improve a student's behaviours also often include the number of the contract).

PREVENTION OF INAPPROPRIATE BEHAVIOURS

Using positive rewards is always more desirable than using even mild forms of punishment. So the teachers may reduce the need to use punishment techniques by preventing many behaviour problems. Lewis and Doorlag (1987) recommend several preventive measures.

1. Make rules and routines positive, concrete and functional, relating them to the accomplishments of learning and order

in the classroom (e.g. "work quietly at the learning centres" rather than" don't talk when working).

2. Design rules and routines to anticipate potential classroom problems and to manage these situations. For example, teachers may want students to raise their hands when they need help rather than calling out or leaving their seat to locate the teacher.
3. Establish classroom rules and routines at the beginning of the school year by introducing them the first day.
4. Demonstrate or model the rules and routines and continue to provide opportunities for students to practise them until the students have mastered them.
5. Associate rules and routines with simple signals that tell students when they are to carry out or stop specific activities or behaviours.
6. Monitor how students follow rules and routines, rewarding students for appropriate behaviour.

The above mentioned behaviour management strategies are teacher directed. There are other effective strategies managed by the student or, in part, by other students. Co-operative learning is one peer-mediated intervention used frequently.

SUMMARY

Emotional/behavioural disorders involve inappropriate social interactions and transactions between the child and social environment. Emotional/behaviour disorder is not simply a problem of undesirable behaviour or inappropriate social circumstances. Most of the children with emotional/behavioural disorders are isolated from others because they either withdraw from social contact or behave in an aggressive, hostile way and others withdraw from them.

Many terms have been used for children's emotional/ behavioural disorders. Children with emotional/behavioural disorders can be defined as those who exhibit inappropriate behaviour to such a marked extent and over a long period of time that it has an adverse effect on educational performance.

Emotional/behavioural disorders can be classified into two dimension as externalising (aggression, acting out) and internalising (immaturity, withdrawal). Six dimensions found in research are conduct disorders, socialised aggression, attention-problems, immaturity, anxiety withdrawal, psychotic behaviour, and motor excesses. Although all children exhibit behaviour characteristics of one or more of these dimensions to some degree, children with emotional/behavioural disorders tend to exhibit this behaviour to an extreme extent.

The major contributing factors of emotional/behavioural disorders are biological conditions, family relationships, cultural influences and school experiences. The common characteristics of children with emotional/behavioural disorders include aggressive behaviour, withdrawn and immature behaviour and hyperactivity.

Children with emotional/behavioural disorders can be easily identified by the teachers by means of careful observation. The most effective identification procedures include a combination of teacher's rankings and ratings and direct observation of student's behaviour. Peer rankings or ratings can also be used well.

Special educational programmes for children with emotional/ behavioural disorder include the psychoanalytic approach, psychoeducational approach, humanistic approach, ecological approach, and behavioural approach. Teaching them in general education classrooms involves increasing appropriate behaviour, decreasing inappropriate behaviour, preventing inappropriate behaviour and learning behaviours they do not know already.

REFERENCES

Hallahan, D.P., and Kauffman, J.M. (1993) *Exceptional Children: Introduction to Special Education.* Prentice-Hall, Englewood Cliffs, NJ.

Lewis, R.B., and Doorlag, D.H. (1987) *Teaching Special Students in the Mainstream.* Chas E Merrill, Columbus, OH.

Slavin, R.E. (1986) *Educational Psychology: Theory into Practice.* Prentice-Hall.

8

GIFTED CHILDREN

OBJECTIVES

This chapter dials with education of gifted children. After reading this chapter, the readers should be able to:

1. Develop an insight into the concept of giftedness.
2. Understand the characteristics of gifted children.
3. Identify gifted children in the classrooms.
4. Define creativity
5. Devise instruction for gifted and creative children.

People who have special gifts, or at least have the potential for gifted performance, may go through life unrecognised. Similarly, sometimes gifted children and youths are not discovered as their families and close associates do not give much importance to their special abilities. Lack of opportunities or training also does not bring them to light. Especially, when the students belong to poor families or minority groups, they may be deprived of chances to demonstrate and develop their potential. We would have more outstanding artists and scientists if every talented child had the opportunity and the training necessary to develop his or her talents to the fullest possible extent. Most of us feel it a moral obligation to help those who are at some disadvantage compared to the average person but we don't feel like so to help gifted children become better. It is on this issue-the desirability and dire necessity of helping our most capable children become even better-that special education for gifted children is likely to founder.

DEFINITION

Children with special gifts are very superior to a comparison group of other children of the some age. Beyond this simple statement there is little agreement about how giftedness should be defined. The disagreements are due primarily to differences of opinion regarding the following questions:

1. In what way are gifted children superior?
2. How is superiority measured?
3. To what degree must a child be superior to be considered gifted?
4. Who should make up the comparison group?

Even the terminology of giftedness is rather confusing. Besides the word "gifted", there are a variety of other terms used to describe individuals who are superior to other children. Such terms are talented, creative, insightful, genius and precocious.

Precocity refers to remarkable early development. Many highly gifted children manifest precocity in particular area of development, such as, language, music, or mathematical ability. The rate of intellectual development of all gifted children exceeds that of non-gifted children.

Insight may be defined as separating relevant from the irrelevant information, finding novel and useful ways of combining relevant bits of information, or relating old and new information in a novel and productive way.

Genius indicates a particular aptitude or capacity in any area. More often, it is used to indicate extremely rare intellectual powers such as extremely high I.Q. or creativity.

Creativity refers to the ability to express novel and useful ideas, to sense and elucidate novel and important relationships, and to ask previously unthought of, but crucial questions.

Talent is a word ordinarily used to indicate special ability, aptitude or accomplishment.

Giftedness refers to cognitive (intellectual) superiority (not necessarily of genius caliber), creativity and motivation in combination and of sufficient magnitude to set the child apart from the vast majority of age mates. These qualities make it possible for gifted children to contribute something of particular value to society.

The traditional definition of giftedness is based on general intelligence test, usually the Stanford Binet, or the Wechsler Intelligence Scale for children Revised. That is, children had traditionally been considered gifted if they scored above a particular level on the Binet or the WISC-R. According to traditional definition, the gifted children are those children whose potential intellectual powers are at a high educational level in both producting and evaluative thinking.

More recently giftedness is conceptualised in terms of developmental model. Giftedness may be thought of as a superior to extraordinary developmental outcome resulting from the joint function of a relatively unimpaired and invulnerable organism and a facilitative environment. That is, children can attain a gifted level of performance only when they are (1) relatively free of biological impairments, (2) mostly invulnerable to environmental stresses that tend to limit performance, and (3) reared in an environment that supports performance.

Gifted children can be defined for purposes of education as those children who demonstrate or manifest potential for high ability including high intelligence, high creativity and high task commitment. The reason for using the multiple-criterion definition is that all these three characteristics-high ability, high creativity and high task commitment-seem to be very necessary for truly gifted performance in any field.

ORIGINS OF GIFTEDNESS

It is not surprising that brilliant parents are more likely to have gifted children than the parents of average or retarded intelligence. It is a known fact that an impoverished environment is less likely to produce gifted children. There may be a few exceptions. Some children of intellectually dull parents may be gifted despite their environmental disadvantages. But the statistical evidence indicates that giftedness increases when the child's parents have higher than average intelligence and provide a better than average environment for the child. The origins of giftedness are not fully understood. Well-designed research works need to be undertaken to discover the relative contribution of genetic and environmental factors to giftedness and the precise nature of the genetic and environmental factors that contribute to giftedness.

GENETIC AND OTHER BIOLOGICAL FACTORS

The proposition that intelligence and highly valued skills are inherited is not a very popular one in our egalitarian society. The fact that giftedness is partly inherited, irrespective the definition proposed, should not be taken as an indication that environmental factors are unimportant. Genetic influences on the development of superior abilities can not be denied, but these biological influences are clearly no more important than the environments in which the children are nurtured.

Biological factors that are not genetic may also contribute to the determination of intelligence. For example, nutritional and neurological factors may to some extent, determine how intellectually competent a child becomes. Severe malnutrition in infancy or childhood, as well as neurological damage at any age, can result in mental retardation. At the same time, it is wrong to assume that superior nutrition and neurological status early in life alone can contribute to superior intelligence.

In conclusion, it may be stated that genetic factors are clearly involved in the determination of giftedness. Environmental factors alone can not account for giftedness of children. It is to be noted that an individual does not inherit an IQ or talent. What is inherited is a collection of genes that along with experiences determine the limits of intelligence and other abilities.

ENVIRONMENTAL FACTORS

There is no doubt that families, schools, communities obviously exercise a profound influence on the development of children's abilities. Stimulation, opportunities, expectations, demands, and rewards for performance affect children's learning. Research works have established that there is a correlation between socioeconomic level and IQ. Influences of home and families, especially in the child's younger years, are extremely important. The following were found to occur in the families of highly successful persons.

- Someone in the family, usually one of the parents, had a personal interest in the child's talent and provided great support and encouragement for its development.
- There was specific parental encouragement for the child to explore, to participate in home activities related to the area of developing talent, and to join the family in related activities. Small signs of interest and capability by the child were rewarded.
- Expected behaviours and values related to the talent were present in the family. Clear schedules and standards for performance appropriate for the child's stage of development were held.
- The family interacted with the tutor/mentor and received information to guide the child's practice.
- Parents observed practice, insisted that the child put in the required amount of practice time, provided instruction where

necessary, and rewarded the child whenever something was done especially well or when a standard was met.

Parents encourage participation in events such as recitals, concerts, contests, etc. in which the child's capabilities were displayed in public.

We may conclude that children who realise their potential for accomplishment well have families that are stimulating, directive, supportive and rewarding of their abilities. Also, the ways in which the schools identify giftedness, group children for instruction, design curricula, and reward performance have a profound effect on what the most able students achieve. Furthermore, striving for upward social mobility and the high value attached to achievement in specific area among certain cultural and ethnic groups also contribute to giftedness.

In summary, it may be stated that environmental influences have much to do with how a child's genetic endowment is expressed in performance. But neither environment nor genetics can be entirely responsible for the performance of gifted or retarded individuals. It is the genetic factors that apparently determine the range within which a person will function, and it is the environmental factors that determine whether the individual will function in the lower or upper reaches of that range.

CHARACTERISTICS OF THE GIFTED CHILDREN

There is no doubt that gifted children exhibit their talents by their remarkable performance in any task undertaken by them. Teachers can easily identify these children by keenly observing their performance. A number of misconceptions are found among laymen regarding their physical stature and social adjustment. Recent researchers have thoroughly studied groups of gifted children and they outline the following as the common characteristics of gifted children.

PHYSICAL CHARACTERISTICS

Gifted children as a group are taller, heavier, stronger, more energetic, and healthier than other children of their age who have average intelligence. It is wrong to assume that all gifted children are physically weak, small, and sickly. Many gifted children have been outstanding in athletic ability and superior competitors in a variety of sports. There are two things to be noted here. First, although the gifted children clearly tend to excel their average age mates in both mental and physical characteristics by the time they are several years old, it is not easily possible to detect their superiority at birth or even during the first year in most cases. Second, since there is a correlation between IQ and socioeconomic status, the apparent physical superiority of gifted children may be a result of nonintellectual factors.

EDUCATIONAL CHARACTERISTICS

Gifted children tend to be far ahead of average children in academic achievement. They learn to read very easily. Many of them are taught to read by parents or teach themselves before they enter school. Many of them are more advanced in reading than in areas that require manual dexterity, such as writing, art. They are more advanced in reading than in math, which depends more on sequential development of concepts and skills. Contrary to common opinion, which pictures gifted children as constantly bored with and antagonistic towards school, most of the gifted children like school very much and they love to learn. Many gifted children are younger than their classmates because of their superior academic performance.

OCCUPATIONAL CHARACTERISTICS

It is not surprising that gifted students tend to enter occupations that demand greater than average intellectual ability, creativity and motivation. Most of them find their ways into the ranks of professionals and managers. A high proportion of gifted children distinguish themselves among their peers in adulthood. As educationally, they are winners occupationally also. But again, it is important to note that this description does not hold true for every gifted student.

SOCIAL AND EMOTIONAL CHARACTERISTICS

Gifted children tend to be happy and well liked by their peers. Most of them are social leaders at school. They are emotionally stable and self-sufficient and are less prone to neurotic and psychotic disorders than average children. They exhibit wide and varied interests and perceive themselves in positive terms. Recent research studies have abetted the misconception that gifted persons tend to be social misfits and emotional cripples. Most societies have a great deal of trouble in dealing with extreme advance of any kind, and someone with an IQ of 180 is certainly unusual. So it is not proper to characterise all extremely gifted people as maladjusted and eccentric.

At the same time, it is not proper to assume that gifted students are immune to social and emotional problems. They are also particularly susceptible to difficulties if they have extremely high IQ or if they are subject to social conditions, such as peer pressure toward mediocrity, that mitigate against mental health. Gifted students become upset and maladjusted when they are discriminated against and prevented from realising their full potential.

MORAL AND ETHICAL CHARACTERISTICS

Most studies show gifted people to be superior to average individuals in concern for moral and ethical issues and in moral behaviour. Even at earlier age, gifted children tend to be concerned with abstract concepts of good and evil, right and wrong, justice and injustice. Gifted persons tend to be particularly concerned with social problems and the ways they can be resolved. Gifted persons are the ones who have the greatest potential for helping individuals and societies resolve their moral and ethical dilemmas. It is worth noting that almost all the definitions of giftedness include people who are recognised as moral giants. However, the corruptibility of high executives in every profession in every society raises questions about the moral and ethical superiority of gifted persons. The atrocities of the Nazis in Germany, some of whom were able, creative, motivated individuals, testify to the fact that gifted and talented people can make criminal use of their potential. The moral and ethical shortcomings of these individuals are not characteristic of gifted people as group. The immoral, unethical gifted individual is an exception rather than the rule.

IDENTIFYING GIFTED CHILDREN

Parents, teachers, psychologists and social workers can help in identifying gifted children at an early stage. It is a problem that has drawn the attention of psychologists and educationists all over the world. They are of the opinion that it is extremely difficult to assess or measure giftedness with the help of a single test or tool. Authorities in this field have proposed various procedures in which there are some overlappings to a considerable extent. Generally intelligence tests and creative tests are administered for identifying giftedness in children. Tests of creativity involve the ability to deal with verbal and numerical symbol systems. In addition to these tests, scholastic achievement tests can also be used to assess giftedness. But the problem is that these tests are not comprehensive or valid enough to assess creativity. We shall discuss identification procedures proposed by some authorities in this field.

RENZULLI AND DELCOURT'S PROCEDURE

Renzulli and Delcourt observe that four criteria are very useful to identify gifted students. The criteria are (1) test scores; (2) academic mastery in specific domains; (3) creative productivity in specific domains or inter-disciplinary areas, with products being assessed by teacher judgement and student interest and willingness to pursue advanced follow-up activities, and (4) long-range creative productivity-the ultimate criterion, which can be used to identify gifted persons only after the fact of their performance. Test scores have been the most widely used criteria. But identification on the basis of testing alone is now widely viewed as inappropriate.

GETZELS' PROCEDURE

Getzels has described the following measures to assess giftedness and creativity.

(i) Word Association Test (WAT): The test presents words to the subjects. Each word has multiple meanings. Here the children taking the tests are required to write as many meanings as he knows for each word. Gifted children usually furnish more meanings than their age mates of average intelligence.

(ii) Uses of Objects: The subjects are expected to write as many different uses for each object as they possibly can. Gifted children are usually able to think of many uses of each object. From that, giftedness of children can be assessed to a considerable extent.

(iii) Hidden Shapes: The children are required to identify the complex figures in which the single figure appears. Gifted children are able to identify more complex figures in less time than their age mates of average intelligence.

(iv) Fables: Here the children are provided with the same fables whose last lines are blank. The children are required to fill in these blanks to form a suitable ending. Here, the gifted children will exhibit their originality and creativity. This will help in identifying gifted and creative children.

(v) Make-up Problems: Here the children are required to use the information given to them to make up as many problems as they can within a limited time span. The gifted children will be able to make up much more problems than their age mates of normal intelligence within the limited time span. Gifted children will exhibit speed and accuracy.

KOUGH AND DE HAON'S PROCEDURE

Kough and De Haon have developed a procedure to discover special abilities and disabilities. Their procedure is very conducive to identify gifted children. They have furnished different criteria to identify special abilities and talents among gifted children. The criteria proposed by them fall under three areas:

(i) Intellectual ability

(ii) Mechanical skills.
(iii) Physical skills

WILLY'S PROCEDURE

Willy has listed out the following procedure for identifying gifted children.

(i) Accuracy and use of vocabulary
(ii) Language proficiency
(iii) Quick, keen observation and retention of information about things.
(iv) Early interest in calendars, in telling time and in clocks.
(v) Quality of concentration.
(vi) The early development of ability to read.

This procedure largely requires keen observation on the part of the teacher and parents. Once these are observed in children, the teacher can administer intelligence test to gifted children for scientific confirmation of giftedness.

SIMPLIFIED PROCEDURE OF PRACTITIONERS

Although the authorities in this field have proposed various procedures, the following three-step procedure is very feasible and conducive to identify gifted children. In this procedure it is the teacher who plays the prominent role. Moreover, the teacher can base his assessment on his daily observation of his students and the students' educational records. This procedure includes.

(i) Observation
(ii) Educational assessment
(iii) Standardised test

(i) Observation

This is the most convenient and practically the foremost technique to identify gifted children. Observation of the children's behaviour by the teacher as well as the experts helps in identifying gifted students. This can be done in simple as well as controllable conditions. While observing the children's behaviour a strict vigil should be kept to study their reactions to various situations. A child's behaviour can be observed not only in classroom, but also on the playground, home and in the group. Observation can be done by just scrupulously watching the child at close quarters and by moving along with the child. How the child grasps the instructional presentation and how he responds in the classroom and in the school premise should be noted down. Observation technique is very useful for ascertaining the curricular, co-curricular, extra-curricular, and recreational interest of the children. In educational programmes such as recitation of a memory poem or reproduction of an essay or passage of testing comprehension or a quiz programme will bring to light the giftedness or the special talent in the children. But observation technique alone will not suffice for reliable identification. So, there is a need to complement observation technique with other tests or tools.

(ii) Educational Assessment

An educational assessment provides a detailed description of the child in the school setting, giving information about:

1. The child's level of attainment in the basic subjects in terms of what he can do, what his special abilities or disabilities appear to be. Evaluation of scholastic achievement is possible through scholastic tests. From the records maintained in the school such as mark sheets, progress cards, and cumulative records the teachers can assess giftedness or special talents of their children.
2. The child's level of language development and speech: Gifted children can be found to be far ahead of their age or classmates in this respect.
3. Standards of achievement in other areas of curriculum, e.g. in art, practical subjects, physical education.
4. Emotional and social behaviour as displayed both in and out of the classroom.
5. Previous school history with particular reference to attitude towards school, their special achievement and laurels.

All the above measures can be undertaken by the teacher with the records available at his disposal. These will bring to light the giftedness or the special abilities in children. Another advantage is that all the records are available at the disposal of the teacher and no service from the experts is required to make an educational assessment of children.

(iii) Standardised Tests

All the gifted children are supposed to have a high IQ. Through the use of many standardised intelligence tests the intellectual level of children can be assessed. There are verbal as well as nonverbal intelligence tests, which can be used for this purpose. But the psychologists prefer individual verbal tests to group verbal tests. It is possible to get a clear picture of the mental capacities of children by administering many intelligence tests. A single test will not suffice to bring out the full picture of mental abilities of a child. Psychologists usually administer more than one standardised test to make an assessment about a child. Terman - Merill Scale, Wechsler Intelligence Scale for Children. Revised, Standard progressive matrices etc are some widely used intelligence tests. For Indian children, nonverbal tests like Raven's Standard Progressive matrices will be very effective. According to Terman-Merill Scale if a child is found to possess an I.Q. of 150 and above he may be termed as gifted. Similarly each test gives specific cutoff line or score for giftedness.

One caution must be sounded here. IQ alone should not be considered a sole criterion for defining giftedness or for identifying gifted children. Standardised tests are tools of formal assessment. This formal assessment should be complemented with informal assessment measures such as observation and educational assessment. One assessment measure without the other can not be very effective. Hence this simplified procedure suggested by us includes three steps representing both formal and informal assessment measures.

ESSENTIALS OF IDENTIFICATION

Even though there are several methods for identifying gifted children, all these methods incorporate the following salient points in their procedures.

- A teacher can perceive indications of giftedness by means of keen observation. The teacher should have adequate competency to interpret what he observes.
- Class marks and different records of student's achievement in the school may provide adequate indications.
- Individual or group intelligence tests are very conducive for identifying gifted children.
- Careful observation should be made for identifying gifted children and the teacher should not depend on a single test for arriving at conclusive decisions.

LIMITATIONS OF IDENTIFICATION TECHNIQUE

There are some limitations of various techniques generally used for identifying gifted children. They are as follows:

1. Intelligence tests are very expensive and time consuming.
2. Group intelligence tests are good for screening. But it is not without drawback. The major drawback is that students having motivational and emotional problems are rarely identified and so are students having reading difficulties.
3. Administration of achievement test batteries fails to identify underachieving gifted children.
4. Children having antagonistic attitude towards school are seldom identified as gifted children. This applies to students having motivational and emotional problems.
5. IQ alone can not be considered a sole criterion for identifying gifted children. Assessment is to be based on some other aspects also, besides IQ.

PREVALENCE

It is assumed that 3 to 5 percent of the school population could be considered gifted or talented. Obviously the prevalence of giftedness is a function of the definition chosen. If giftedness is defined as the top x percent on a given criterion, the question of prevalence can be answered. When IQ is used as the sole or primary criterion for giftedness, more children will come from homes of higher IQ economic status with fewer siblings and better educated parents. But gifted children are not distributed equally across all social classes when IQ is the primary means of identification. So IQ alone can not be considered a sufficient or valid criterion for defining giftedness and for identifying gifted children.

Renzulli argues convincingly that the assumption that only 3 to 5 percent of the school population are gifted is needlessly restrictive and may result in many potentially gifted students' contributions being overlooked. He is of the opinion that 15 to 25 percent of all children may have adequate ability, motivation, and creativity to exhibit gifted behaviour at some time during their school career.

EDUCATION FOR GIFTED CHILDREN

It is relatively easy to find sympathy for handicapped children, and more than a little difficult to turn that sympathy into public support for effective educational programmes. On the other hand, it is very difficult to elicit sympathy for gifted children, and next to impossible to arrange sustained public support for education that meets their needs. Generally, gifted children face a number of problems when they attend regular classes. Usually, in the mainstream classes the educational programmes are planned and devised for children of average ability. When the gifted children are admitted to these classes, they are denied the opportunities they need for full development of their talents. As such, their education is restricted. The teacher also miserably fails to devise his instruction so as to accommodate individual differences. The worst sufferers in this respect are the gifted children.

WHY SPECIAL EDUCATION FOR GIFTED CHILDREN

The gifted children are very often allowed double promotions, which places the bright children in a senior class. It is done with an assumption that the bright child will be able to find a challenge in the work of a senior class and make use of his talents. But this is not a healthy and desirable practice. When a child is given an accelerated promotion, he is placed out of his own group with respect to physical, social and emotional development. Research evidence indicates that when a child is placed with children who are higher in the developmental continuum, he usually finds himself out of step in other activities and interests. So in stead of giving accelerated promotion, the gifted student can be provided with enriched programmes while he is allowed to share the experiences of children of his own level of development.

It is a common practice in school to entrust more works to gifted children. It is not a desirable practice. It is important to note that when these students are overlooked with a mediocre type of work, it causes monotony and boredom. Giving more works is not a sign of enrichment. It is only quantitative improvement. What is needed here is qualitative improvement. The works given to these children must be challenging to them. The teacher should avoid giving them routine type of work. Gifted children want to accomplish difficult tasks, which pose challenges to them and which they can complete independently. When they investigate for themselves, it givens them a sense of satisfaction. Enrichment programme does not include repetition and drill, which are considered to be effective for backward children. But they tend to irritate the gifted students and affect their performance seriously.

When these students are not provided with enriched educational programmes, there is likelihood for them to develop bad social habits. When the task given to them is not challenging and satisfying they tend to engage themselves in loafing and indulging in antisocial activities for excitement. When the teacher plans his work for average children, the gifted students become frustrated and they invite disciplinary problems in the classroom. When other children need one full period to complete the given assignment, gifted children will be able to accomplish it in less than half the time and they want to utilise the available extra time in an interesting way. But act of gifted children is not usually appreciated by the teachers who get distracted from their attention to majority children.

Sometimes the curriculum is planned in such a way that it would miss some of the aspects of the developments of a child. Gifted children need ample opportunities for an all round development of their personality. Hence, enrichment of the educational programme should include development of the social, aesthetic and emotional aspects of personality in addition to academic aspects. The enriched programme must be suitable for individual needs, demands, and nature of development.

EDUCATIONAL PROGRAMMES OF GIFTED CHILDREN

(1) An educational programme devised for the benefit of gifted students should include the following characteristics:

A curriculum designed to accommodate the students' advanced cognitive skills, (2) instructional strategies consistent with the learning styles of gifted students in the particular content areas, and (3) administrative arrangements facilitating appropriate grouping of students for instruction. Generally, the plans can be described as providing for the following measures.

(i) Enrichment.
(ii) Acceleration, and
(iii) Grouping in Special classes

ENRICHMENT

Enrichment refers to provision of a differentiated programme of study for gifted students by the classroom teacher within the regular classroom, without assistance from an outside resource or consultant teacher. Additional experiences are provided to the gifted students without placing them in a higher grade.

MODELS OF ENRICHMENT

There are a few models of enrichment proposed by educators. One model of enrichment that has received widespread attention is the "Revolving Door Model". This model is based on the notion that children manifest gifted behaviour in relation to particular projects or activities on which they bring to bear their above average ability, creativity, and task commitment. Students are selected to constitute a "talent pool" through case study identification methods. These students are engaged in enrichment activities that involve individual to small group investigation of real life problems. They become participating pollsters, politicians, geologists, editors, and so on. The teacher should help students translate and focus a general concern into a solvable problem and provide the students with required tools and methods to solve the problem. Further, he should assist the students in communicating their findings to authentic audiences. Students can stay in the enrichment programme as long as they have the ability, creativity, and motivation to pursue productive activities that go beyond the usual curriculum for students of their age.

8.1. MAJOR COMPONENTS OF SCHOOLWIDE ENRICHMENT MODEL

Curriculum Compacting. Modifying or "streamlining" the regular curriculum in order to eliminate repetition of previously mastered material, upgrade the challenge level of the regular curriculum, and provide time for appropriate enrichment and/or acceleration activities while ensuring mastery if basic skills.

Assessment of Student Strengths. A systematic procedure for gathering and recording information about student's abilities, interests, and learning styles.

Type I Enrichment: General Exploratory Experiences. Experiences and activities that are designed to expose students to a wide variety of disciplines (fields of study), visual and performing arts, topics, issues, occupations, hobbies, persons, places, and events that are not ordinarily covered in the regular curriculum.

Type II Enrichment: Group Training Activities. Instructional methods and materials that are purposefully designed to promote the development of thinking and feeling processes.

Type III Enrichment: Individual and Small Group Investigations of Real Problems. Investigative activities and artistic productions in which the learner assumes the role of a first hand inquirer, the student thinking, feeling, and acting like a practising professional.

A school wide enrichment model has been developed more recently. The school-wide model was designed to reduce the "separateness" of special and regular programmes and to make certain that all students who can profit from enrichment activities are given opportunities to engage in more challenging activities. The objectives of "curriculum compacting" are to create a challenging learning environment, guarantee proficiency in basic curriculum and make time for enrichment and acceleration. All the students' strengths are assessed. Type I enrichment provides general exploratory experiences. Type II Enrichment comprises group training activities, and Type III Enrichment incorporates individual and small-group investigations of real problems.

Research evidence suggests that this school-wide enrichment model can improve the learning environment for all the students. Also, it improves the attitude of the students and teachers towards education of the gifted and makes special programming for gifted students a more integral part of general education. These outcomes disclose the effectiveness of special programmes for the gifted students. The gains that the gifted education has made in instructional technology and the commitment that this field has made to serving out most potentially able youth well will only have long-term endurance when they are woven into the fabric of general education.

ACCELERATION

Acceleration contributes to academic achievement. No negative effects on social or emotional development have been established. If at all any adjustment problems occur, they tend to be minor and temporary in nature. On the other hand, failure to advance a precocious child may result in poor study habits, apathy, lack of motivation, and maladjustment. Those who argue against acceleration are of the firm opinion that the children who are grouped with older students will suffer negative social and emotional consequences or that they will become contemptuous of their age-peers. While the opponents of acceleration argue like this, the proponents argue that by being grouped with older students who are their intellectual peers in classes in which they are not always first or correct, the gifted students acquire a more realistic self-concept and learn tolerance for others of inferior abilities. So far, the research evidence seems clearly to support acceleration, especially in the case of the most gifted students.

GROUPING IN SPECIAL CLASSES

Psychologists and educationists recognise the need for special classes and school for the education of gifted children. These classes are called elite classes. Researchers have established the efficacy of special classes. Still the situation is not so simple as it is thought to be. The debate on desirability of special education for the gifted is still going on. There are strong arguments for and against special classes and schools. Some of the points advanced by the proponents of special classes are as follows:

1. The task assigned to average children in regular classes is not adequate for the gifted children. They are restrained to a great extent. On the other hand, in a special class they are provided with enriched activities to work according to their superior ability. Another pertinent fact is that special class provides for mutual stimulation, which induces the gifted children to progress and develop more rapidly.
2. Placing gifted children in regular classrooms tends to develop some careless habits in them. The gifted children find the task given to then very easy and sometimes they don't feel like working them out. This may lead to indiscipline and maladjustment. On the other hand, the special classes offer challenging tasks to gifted children and enable the children to develop their potentialities to the maximum.
3. Where there is no provision for special classes, the gifted children are given accelerated promotion. This method forces the gifted children to learn with more mature and older children. A point to be noted in accelerated promotion is that a superior child may not necessarily be superior in sociality and other aspects of development. As a result, he may face some problems of social adjustment. There is no such problem in special classes where they have the scope for passing grades at normal rate and opportunity to move with his own ability group.
4. In the regular classroom the tasks assigned to the entire class are much simple for gifted students who finish them much quicker than in the anticipated time span. This leave them with time to spare till the average children complete the tasks. In the meantime, the alert mind of gifted children is diverted to seek some other outlet. This warrants special classes for gifted children where they can be provided with enriched activities to keep them at desk and on the job during the entire time span.

5. The empirical works in this area indicate that special classes also provide ample opportunities to develop leadership qualities in various arenas. There may be some children specially gifted in painting, poetry mathematics, literature and other branches of knowledge. More developed and well-planned programmes can facilitate manifestation of their special talent and their emergence as prominent ones in these particular fields.
6. It is rightly pointed out that gifted children are made of finer stuff than the majority of children. These children are more sensitive, alert, and quick in their thinking. If proper stimulation is not provided to these children, they tend to create problems in the class. When these children are put together with the average group, an inferior ability group, the teacher finds it very difficult to devise his instruction so as to accommodate both the groups. Treatment and handling of these two types of groups become very difficult for teacher. If the either group is given importance, the other is neglected.

Although the above arguments have been advanced by the proponents of special classes, the opponents of special classes also advance some points against the special classes. Those psychologists and educationists, who oppose special classes, strongly refute the isolation or segregation of gifted children from regular schools. They have their own reasons. These reasons should be taken as constructive criticisms of the move. The counter arguments advanced by the opponents of special classes for gifted children are as follows:

1. The potent criticism against special class for gifted children is that it is highly undemocratic. Equal opportunity of education should be provided to one and all.
2. There is a striking possibility for gifted children to develop conceit, if they are taken away from regular classes. They become more aware of their superior ability and fail to develop modesty as personality trait.
3. Special classes give rise to a kind of intellectual aristocracy. The segregation of gifted children and formation of special ability groups give rise to ideas of superiority.
4. Isolation of gifted children from regular class affects the average children very much. While learning with gifted children, average children get ample opportunities to learn

many things. Withdrawal of gifted children from regular class deprives the average children of rich stimulation.

5. Special class programme deprives the society of superior leadership. While working with average children, the gifted children get chances to act as leaders and get training in leadership. This in the long run, provides the society with good leaders.
6. The most important criticism levelled against special education is the high cost of such programmes. When there is not enough money, especially in a developing country like India, for the education of majority average children such expensive programme for the gifted children is least desirable.

TEACHING GIFTED STUDENTS IN GENERAL EDUCATION CLASSROOM

Gifted students who demonstrate gifted behavior are superior in someway, and exhibit abilities and sensitivities that make them express themselves in special ways, learn quickly, be self-sufficient; or understand their own and others' feelings, motivations, and strengths and weaknesses. So, the classroom teachers should assume the responsibility during most of the school day for providing the educational experiences for gifted and talented students. There are certain techniques that have been verified to be effective in teaching gifted and talented students in general education classrooms. Some of the techniques that teachers can try for teaching gifted and talented students are discussed below.

SELF-DIRECTED LEARNING

One type of experience that benefits the academically gifted students is self-directed learning, which helps students move systematically from teacher determined and directed instruction towards independent learning. The main goals of self-directed learning are as follows.

1. Learning to function effectively in one's total environment.
2. Learning to make choice and decisions based on self-knowledge of needs and interests.

3. Learning to assume responsibility for choices and decisions by completing all activities at a satisfactory level of achievement and in an acceptable time frame.
4. Learning to define problems and to determine a course of action for their solution; and
5. Learning to evaluate one's own work.

The proponents of self-directed learning programme believe that the process of self-directed learning culminates in students being able to initiate plans for their own learning, identify resources, gather data, and develop and evaluate their own products and projects. There are a variety of techniques such as curriculum compacting, learning centres, independent study, and contracting to promote self-directed learning in the general education classes at all grade levels. A brief discussion of each of these techniques is presented here.

CURRICULUM COMPACTING

Curriculum compacting is a procedure in which the teacher modifies the regular curriculum to provide additional time for gifted students to pursue alternative learning activities. These modifications must be made based on the strengths of the gifted students, using a variety of information sources such as school records, previous teacher recommendations, standardised and informal tests results, and observation. After deciding what curricular areas are most appropriate for compacting, the following questions should be considered.

1. What does the student already know?
2. What does the student need to learn?
3. What activities will meet the students' learning needs?

Having made these assessment and instructional decisions, the teacher must decide how to provide appropriate alternative educational activities.

LEARNING CENTRES

Teachers can make use of learning centres to provide the gifted students with enrichment activities. These centres must offer instructional opportunities in areas that are specifically designed and sequenced to encourage student independence. This will promote self-directed learning. Interest development centres also can be designed by teachers to offer activities that develop productivity and creativity of their gifted students. While the traditional learning centres help students master basic curriculum skills, interest development centres (IDCs) facilitate students' exploration of a wide range of topics not included in the regular curriculum. The centres must have adequate manipulative, and media and print materials along with several suggestions for examining and experimenting in special interest areas.

INDEPENDENT STUDY

Sometimes students will develop great interest in a topic they have explored. When the gifted students develop such interest, the teacher should encourage them to conduct an independent study on their topics of interest. Independent study involves not only the exploration of a topic in depth but also the production of an original report that is disseminated to an appropriate audience. Directing independent study is time consuming and it requires an understanding of the topic. So the teachers often seek the help of a resource teacher and another person who is knowledgeable about the subject and willing to participate in the project. The role of the teacher and resource person(s) is not to be director of the study; rather, they serve as assistants who help the students. They should offer specific helps to students to

1. Define and frame the problem.
2. Establish realistic goals and time lines
3. Become aware of a variety of useable resources.
4. Identify both a product that the study will produce and an audience for the product.
5. Make a self-evaluation of their study.

In addition, the adults involved in the project must reinforce the students' work throughout the study and provide methodological help when necessary.

CONTRACTS

Teachers can facilitate self-directed learning by providing individualised exploration and instruction in the form of student contracts. Like business contracts, these documents are negotiated with the students and describe the area each student will study and procedures and resources he or she will use in the investigation. Contracts are used to guide independent study. Also, the contracts can specify the intended audience, the means of dissemination, deadlines for stages or steps in the study, and dates and purposes of periodic meetings with the teacher.

Thus the teachers can teach gifted and creative students in general education classroom. The teacher must be a source of inspiration and encouragement. He must provide opportunities as discussed above, to gifted children to test their potentialities and to explore more avenues. When the teacher provides for self-directed learning, it benefits both the gifted and the average children. It benefits the gifted children in the sense that it enables them to work to their potentials, and it benefits the average children in that the interactions and disseminations of gifted students provide adequate stimulation and motivation to average students for better acquisition of knowledge and realisation of educational objectives.

SUMMARY

Children with special gifts are very superior to a comparison group of other children of the same age group. Beyond this simple statement there is little agreement about how giftedness should be defined. Giftedness refers to cognitive (intellectual) superiority (not necessarily of genies caliber) creativity and motivation in combination and of sufficient magnitude to set the child apart from the vast majority of age mates.

Gifted children can be defined for purposes of education as those children who demonstrate or manifest potential for high ability including high intelligence, high creativity and high task commitment.

Causes of giftedness include genetic and other biological factors and environmental factors. Major characteristics of gifted children include higher intellectual ability, superior academic performance, creativity and achievement motivation, emotional stability, and good moral behaviour.

Gifted children can be identified on the basis of Renzulli and Delcourt's procedure. The criteria are test (1) test scores, (2) academic mastery, (3) creative productivity, and (4) long range productivity. They can be identified on the basis of Getzel's procedure or on the basis of Kough and DeHaon's procedure also. Simplified procedure includes observation, educational assessment, and standardised tests.

An educational programme devised for the benefit of gifted children should include the following characteristics: (1) a curriculum designed to accommodate the students' advanced cognitive skills (2) instructional strategies consistent with the learning styles of gifted students in the particular content areas, and (3) administrative arrangements. Generally the plan should provide for enrichment, acceleration and grouping in special classes.

To teach gifted children effectively in general education classrooms, teacher can follow useful techniques such as curriculum compacting, providing enrichment learning centre, promoting independent study, and making contracts

REFERENCES

Chintamani Kar (1992) *Exceptional Children: Their Psychology and Instruction.* Sterling Publishers, New Delhi.

Hallahan, D.P., and Kauffman, J.M. (1991) *Exceptional Children: Introduction to Special Education.* Prentice Hall, London.

Renzulli, J.S. (1977) *The Enrichment Triad Model.* Creative learning Press, Wethersfield, CT.

9

INCLUSIVE EDUCATION

OBJECTIVES

This chapter deals with the concept of inclusive education. After reading this chapter, the readers should be able to:

1. Understand the concept of inclusive education.
2. Distinguish between inclusive education and exclusive education.
3. Understand the need for inclusive education.
4. Design educational programmes so as to reach out to all the learners.

The idea of inclusive education is gaining ground all over the world. It was given further impetus by the UNESCO World Conference on Special Needs Education, held in Salamanca, Spain in 1994. The conference considered the future direction of the special needs field in the light of international efforts to ensure the rights of all children to receive basic education. The conference specifically examined how far special needs is part of this 'Education for All' movement. The too confronting questions are: should we aim for a unified system of schooling that is capable of responding to all children as individuals, or should use continue with the tradition of parallel systems whereby some children have separate forms of education?

CONCEPT OF INCLUSION AND EXCLUSION

Inclusive education can be defined as the process of increasing the participation of students in the cultures, curricula, and communities of local mainstream schools whereas exclusive education is the process of reducing the participation. The concepts of participation, culture, curriculum, community and locality require careful analysis. The study of inclusion and exclusion involves the engagement with, and analysis of all students and staff within a school. Inclusive education is concerned with reducing all exclusionary pressures, on the basis of disability, ability, race, gender, class, family structure, lifestyle or sexurability.

The process of inclusion and exclusion are inextricably linked. An analysis of pressures towards exclusion is very important to understand inclusion. It is because within a simple school the same students may be both encouraged and discouraged from participation. All schools, respond to the diversity of their students with a mixture of including and excluding measures, in terms of who they admit to the school, now students are Categorised, grouped and discipline, how teaching and learning is organised, how resources are used, how students who experience difficulties are supported, and how curricula and teaching is developed so that such difficulties are reduced (Booth, Ainscow, Dyson, 1997).

When the students seen as having special needs are integrated into mainstream schools, the teachers tend to adopt practices derived from experiences in special education. Many of these approaches are simply not feasible in primary and secondary schools. These approaches dot not fit with the ways in which mainstream teachers' plan and go about their work. The teachers have to plan for the whole class. Apart from many other consideration, the large number of students in the class as well as the intensity of the teacher's day makes this inevitable.

Therefore the task becomes one of developing the work of the school in response to pupil diversity. Ainscow (1997) notes that this has to include a consideration of overall organisation, curriculum, and classroom practice, support for learning and staff development. There is an increasing amount of evidence from various countries suggesting that measures school take to cater for pupil diversity can lead to more effective form of education for the pupils.

EDUCATIONAL DIFFICULTIES IN INCLUSIVE EDUCATION

Ainscow and Hart (1992) map out some possible perspectives. These perspectives are attempts to characterise alternative ways of looking at the phenomenon of educational difficulty, based on different sets of assumptions that lead to different explanations/different frames of references and different kinds of questions to be addressed. In this sense they lead to assumptions that provide the basis of different theoretical positions.

CHARACTERISTICS OF INDIVIDUAL PUPILS

The first perspective seeks to explain educational difficulties in terms of the characteristics of individual pupils. This remains the dominant perspective in the special needs field, where the nature of educational difficulties is explained in terms of particular disabilities, social background, and/or psychological attributes. The frame of reference created by this perspective is the individual child, and responses are chosen that seek to change or support the child in order to facilitate participation in the process of schooling. Traditionally responses have taken the form of removal of the child from the mainstream curriculum for specialist help. But in the inclusive education system responses have begun to develop which allow help to be provided in the context of the regular classroom.

MISMATCH

The second perspective explains educational difficulties in terms of a mismatch between the characteristics of a particular children and the organisation and/or curriculum arrangements made for them (e.g. Wedell, 1981; Dessent, 1987). Here support is directed towards helping the child to meet the demands and expectations of the system if this is assumed to be fixed or for the time being at least unchangeable. It may to directed towards making modifications to the system in order to extend to range of pupils that can be accommodated. In may respects current 'state of the art' responses (e.g. whole school approaches, differentiation) are informed by this perspective. Further, it is a perspective that is seen as arising as a result of dissatisfaction with the first perspective, which is seen as being a deficit model (Dyson, 1990).

The frame of reference in this interactive perspective once again focuses attention on individual pupils but this time is concerned with the ways they interact with particular contexts and experiences. So much so that those adopting this perspective have tended to argue for the use of the term 'individual needs' rather than 'special needs' (Ainscow and Muncey, 1988). Responses chosen in the light of this perspective includes, curriculum adaptations, alternative materials for pupils, or extra support in the classroom. Sometimes, these responses are also seen as being of benefit to pupils other than those designated as having special needs.

CURRICULUM LIMITATIONS

The third perspective explains educational difficulties in terms of curriculum limitations, using the term curriculum in a broad sense to include all the planned and, indeed unplanned experiences offered to pupils. Thus in this perspective there is a concern with what can be learnt from the difficulties experienced by some children about the limitations of provision currently made for all pupils. The assumption is that changes introduced for the benefit those experiencing difficulties can improve learning for all children (Hart, 1992).

Those adopting this perspective are critical of the limitations of an individual frame of reference even where this is used to raise questions about the adequacy of curriculum organisation and practice as currently provided for individual pupils. They argue that a wider frame is needed, focusing on curriculum organisation and practice as currently provided for all pupils. The task involves continually seeking ways of improving overall conditions for learning, with difficulties acting as indicators of how improvements might be achieved (Ainscow, 1994). Those who adopt this perspective are likely to favour approaches that encourage enquiry as a means of achieving improvement, e.g., various forms of partnership teaching, action research.

It is important to recognise at this stage in the argument that whilst the adoption of a particular perspective tends to encourage the choice of certain types of organisational and curriculum responses, the responses are in themselves often natural as to their orientation. So, for example, support teaching, which has become a very fashionable response to special needs in recent years, might be used by teachers favouring any of these three perspectives. In this case, those adopting a characteristics perspective would see support teaching as a means of providing an individual pupil with extra teaching, albeit in the context or frame work of regular classroom activities, those who take an interactive view, on the other hand, would see support teaching as a way of making modifications to existing arrangements in order to accommodate certain pupils experiencing learning difficulties, whereas the curriculum limitations perspective would encourage the idea that additional adults could facilitate the review and development of existing arrangements in the light of a scrunity of the difficulties experienced by certain pupils.

EDUCATIONAL CONSIDERATIONS

Specific teaching techniques to be adopted to teach children with special needs have been discussed in earlier chapter. In this section, the educational programmes considered to be applicable to inclusive education are briefly discussed. It is still a new field. So there are no tested methods and techniques. Researchers have frequently visited inclusive schools and they have frequently observed the students, staff and their interactions in the actual classrooms. Moreover, they have made exhaustive interviews. On the basis of their observations and interviews of pupils, teachers and parents some programmes have been found to be effective.

ENCOURAGING PARTICIPATION

Teachers must be purposeful, enthusiastic and clear in their directions and instructions to promote greater participation of students. Since the excluded are included in the classroom the teachers must make efforts to link lesson experience to the students' experience to enhance their understanding. For example, while teaching a geography lesson about the Amazon Forests, the teacher can get the class to transform what they already know, mainly, as result of watching American films and TV programmes. All students' contribution must be treated as of equal importance. It will boost up the self-image of the excluded included in the classroom.

Teachers can use specific techniques at various stages of the lesson to encourage engagement with the content and activities. Deliberate use of group-work and collaborative learning strategies between students as they carry out their task will ensure better participation. Encouraging students to be a resource for each other's learning is a further way to increase the classroom teaching resources. Planned group-work provides opportunity for students experiencing difficulties to participate, at least in part of the lesson, without close adult supervision. Non-disabled students can be motivated to opt on their own initiative to work along side and assist students experiencing difficulties.

FORMAL PLANNING

Planning should talk into account all the children in the class. At the same time, the planner has to take account of the content of the individual curriculum plan' that is prepared for each child. Thus the overall programme must cover the whole group whilst at the same time having the flexibility to take account of each child's stage of learning. Children can be encouraged to choose for themselves the order in which they will carry out their assigned tasks, using an individual record sheet to help them plan and report this work.

Formal planning is very important in inclusive education. The formal planning has two elements. First of all there is the planning of the overall learning environment. This involves taking the programmes of the study outlined in the national curriculum and, whilst bearing in mind the principles upon which the school attempts to operate, turning these into appropriate activities, materials and classroom management. The second element is concerned with planning for individuals. This requires the creation of individual curriculum plans for each child based upon the best available knowledge amongst the staff team working with the child. This approach incorporates the notion of individual planning that is so familiar in special education settings but in a way that related to the needs of all children. In a sense it is an approach that implies every child is regarded as being special (Ainscow, 1996).

This formal planning carried out in a collaborative way within the teams provides a basis for yet a third form of planning, influenced by the ideas of Schon (1987). Mel Ainscow (1996) characterises it as planning in action. Planning in action is a demanding requirement on those who work in the school. The heavy emphasis placed on teamwork and collaborations provides on-going support and encouragement for individual staff members. Besides planning, creating flexible and accessible working environment also facilitates pupil participation and learning.

OVERCOMING BARRIERS TO LEARNING

Adult support to overcome problems of participation must be provided in lessons for students categorised as having 'special needs'. It must involve adapting or giving access to the curriculum for individual students. Teachers should have specialisation in 'literacy difficulties', severe learning difficulty, or visual disability. Teachers supporting students with severe learning difficulties must sit with an individual student or a couple of students in a lesson. The teacher can introduce the lesson to the students who may then be asked to work specially prepared materials related to the lesson content. This process will enable students with learning difficulties to learn better. Similarly there may be students with visual difficulties in the inclusive classroom. The approach to teach students with visual difficulties should encourage the students to be independent. Adapted materials must be available to the students at the start of a lesson in order to enable these students to engage in the same activities as others in the class. These programmes have been effectively used with encouraging positive results at Richard Lovell Community High School in U.K.

RESPONDING BY CATEGORY

A traditional category system divided the students into 'mainstream' and 'special'. They were labelled according to their perceived severity of 'need' and the completion of formal procedures as, learning difficulty, or special need without a statement' and 'special need with a statement'. Within the last group, there were a number of sub-groups, including students categorised as having visual difficulties, emotional and behavioural difficulties and learning difficulties.

The model support which arises from the categorisation of some students as having 'special educational needs' has a number of consequences, the educational and social experiences of some 'special' students may be markedly different from those of their peers: the additional resource is provided for a relatively small number of students, leaving little or nothing for those students whose difficulties are not categorised. Further, the 'special needs work' has no obvious means of engaging with and developing ordinary classrooms to become responsive to diversity of all learners. The responsibilities of the co-ordinator of 'special educational needs' for 'special' provision consume all his or her time and energy and prevent him or her and others in the department from working with subject teacher colleagues to develop curricular and teaching approaches for all students

(Gains and McNicholas, 1979; Booth, Potts, and Swann, 1987; Dyson and Gains, 1995).

RESPONSES TO AGE

Most schools cut down student diversity by grouping students by age. Age carries expectations of increasing attainment and maturity. In the English system, students are very rarely allowed to advance a year or to be retained for an extra year. But it is not so in many of the developing countries. So response to age becomes a factor to be reckoned with. Students can be grouped on the basis of age as juniors, seniors and superseniors. Curriculum must be framed somewhat differently for each of these phases. Each of these three phases must have its own head, together with a team of teachers who can take some specific responsibility for the students in that phase. Appointment of Assistant Headmasters for each level in Indian Higher Secondary schools can be made functional in tune with this system.

TEACHING AND LESSONS

A good lesson is when it is all set out on the board and the students get it done in their own time rather than the teacher telling them they have got ten minutes to get this done. Teachers should know the students first before they start teaching the lessons. Knowing the learner well is more important than knowing the lesson to be taught, well. Ample opportunities must be provided to the students to pursue individual projects in some detail over an extended period of time. This approach is in fact valuable. Group work is also of much value for it has capacity to facilitate the students' learning as well as enabling students to further widen their social contracts. Group work in almost every lesson will yield good results. Teacher should encourage optimum interaction in his classroom. Teachers must talk with the students, not talk at them. Teachers' manners and relationship and their respect for students are some factors of prime importance. Explanations are important feature of lessons. Effective teaching involves making the purpose of the task clear and explaining how they should be carried out, whereas unsatisfactory teaching will leave students uncertain or even confused. Students in need of help may be removed from certain lessons to receive individual help in small remedial groups.

BEHAVIOUR AND CONTROL

In U.K. in inclusive education schools they have adopted a system known as 'positive behaviour'. This system consists a set of classroom rules placed prominently in every classroom. There are cumulative rewards and punishments called consequences for adhering to the rules and breaking them. Rewards consist of credits, certificates and prizes. Punishments start with a name on the board, against which ticks can be placed leading on to detention, exclusion from classes and exclusion from the school. There is also a system of informal exclusion known as 'parent referral whereby a student can be sent home with letter to parents. Formal exclusion in accordance with procedures laid down in law can be fixed term, though for no more than five days on anyone occasion, or permanent with guaranteed rights of appeal to parents.

- Teachers should not vary their treatment from pupil to pupil.
- They should ensure that the bright students do not look down upon or ridicule the students with special needs.
- Teachers should be sympathetic with all the students in general, and with students with special needs in particular. At the same time they should be harsh when the situation demands.

HELP AND SUPPORT

Students willingly admit to their own areas of difficulty and need someone they can turn to for help. To serve this purpose there may be a school council for providing the students with counselling and guidance. The students can take their grievances to this school council. The presence of additional adult helpers in some lessons will yield better results. It is likely that the presence of large team of support personnel to support students said to have special needs may also have a wider impact on feelings of being supported. Finally, there is the significant proportion of students with disabilities who, by their very presence, may impact upon relationships and overall climate.

ACCEPTANCE

A good interpersonal relationship is very essential. Similarly there should be a cordial relationship between the students and the teachers. A good relationship prevailing in the school can encourage the climate of support discussed above. Good relationships are always positively influential. There must be a sense of acceptance of differences among the students. This sense of acceptance manifests itself in a variety of forms. There should not be any discrimination on the grounds of caste, creed and colour. In the inclusive education system there are more possibilities for acceptance of students with disabilities as being just part of the normal school community. This acceptance helps the children with disabilities cope a bit more. It is the duty of the teacher to ensure that a sense of acceptance prevails in his classroom besides his accepting all students alike.

The aforesaid programmes are, in fact, very sketchy. They are mostly based on the findings of the research scholars. These scholars observed ' Richard Lovell' Community High School' and 'Eastside School' and found the programmes discussed above to have been effective. Some more thoughts and practices forthcoming in the near future will provide us with further enlightenment.

SUMMARY

The idea of inclusive education is gaining ground all over the world. Inclusive education can be defined as the process of increasing the participation of students in the cultures, curricula, and communities of local mainstream schools whereas exclusive education is the process of reducing the participation.

There are three perspectives on educational difficulties. The first perspective seeks to explain educational difficulties in term of the characteristics of individual pupils. The second perspective explains educational difficulties in terms of a mismatch between the particular characteristics of particular children and the organisation and/or curriculum arrangements made for them. The third perspective explains educational difficulties in terms of curriculum limitations.

Educational consideration in the inclusive education system includes encouraging participation, formal planning, overcoming barriers to learning, responding by category, responses to age, teaching, positive behaviour, help and support, and importance of acceptance.

REFERENCE

Ainscow, M. (1994) *Special Needs in the Classroom: A Teacher Education Guide.* UNESCO, London

Ainscow, M. (1996) *The Development of Inclusive Practices in an English Primary School: Constraints and Influences.* Paper presented at the American Educational Research Association Meeting, New York.

Ainscow, M. (1997) *Towards Inclusive Education* Times Educational Supplement, November 1996.

Ainscow, M. (1998) *Reaching out to All Learners.* Keynote address made at the International conference on School Effectiveness and improvement, Manchester, January 1998.

Ainscow, M., and Hart, S. (1992) Moving Practice Forward *Support for Learning* 7(3), 115 - 120.

Ainscow, M., and Muncey, J. (1989) *Meeting Individual Needs in the Primary School* Fulton, London.

Booth, T., Ainscow, M., and Dyson, A. (1997) understanding Inclusion in a Competitive System. In T. Booth and M. Ainscow (Eds) *From Them to Us. International Voices of Inclusion in Education.* Routeledge, London.

Dessent, T. (1987) *Making the Ordinary School Special.* Flamer, London.

Dyson, A. (1990) Special Educational Needs and the Concept of Change. *Oxford Review of Education.* London

Dyson, A., and Gains, C. (1995) The Special Educational Needs Co-ordinator. *Support For Learning* (Special Issue) 10(2).

Gains, C., and Mc Nicholas, J.A. (1979) *Remedial Education: Guidelines for the Future.* Loryman, London.

Hart, S. (1992) Differentiation Part of the Problem or Part of the Solution? *The Curriculum Journal*, B (2), 131 - 142.

Schon, D.A. (1987) *Educating the Reflective Practitioner*. Jossey - Bass, San Francisco.

Wedell, K. (1981) Concepts of Special Educational Needs. *Education Today*. 31(1), 3- 9.

•••

INDEX